FEMME FRIDAY

Celebrating the Women in the Sherlock Holmes Canon and Transformative Works

Essays by The Baker Street Babes and Friends
Edited by Maria Fleischhack

TABLE OF CONTENTS

ACKNOWLEDGEMENTS

INTRODUCTION

THE LADIES   1

Irene Adler by Lyndsay Faye   2

Maud Bellamy by Fabienne Courouge   5

Lady Mary Brackenstall by Ashley D. Polasek   8

Lady Frances Carfax by Emma Schlimgen-Rozinka   10

Anna Coram by Katie Magnusson   12

Elsie Cubitt by Tamar Zeffren   15

Sally Donovan by Amy Thomas   17

Grace Dunbar by Kristina "Curly" Manente   22

Mrs. Ferguson by Evadare Volney   25

Olivia Flaversham by Kristina "Curly" Manente   28

Annie Harrison by Claire Stemp   30

Eurus Holmes by Amy Thomas   33

Molly Hooper by Amy Thomas   37

Lady Hilda Trelawney Hope by Lyndsay Faye   41

Rachel Howells by Fabienne Courouge   44

Mrs. Hudson by Maria Fleischhack   47

Violet Hunter by Sarah Roy   50

The Irregular Girls by Amy Thomas   53

Isadora Klein by Alexandra Christian   55

Martha by Maria Fleischhack   58

Mary Morstan by Lyndsay Faye   61

Effie Munro and her Daughter Lucy Hebron by Amy Thomas   67

Mary Russell by Ardy   71

Mrs. Ronder by Ro Gorczyca   76

Ettie Schafter by Maria Fleischhack   79

Violet Smith by Melinda Caric   83

Beryl Stapleton by Ashley D. Polasek   86

Mrs. St. Clair by Ashley D. Polasek   90

Helen Stoner by Taylor Blumenberg   92

Mary Sutherland by Elinor Gray   95

Joan Watson by Melinda Caric   98

Kate Whitney Susanne Wagner   100

Kitty Winter by Lyndsay Faye   102

A NOTE ON THE ILLUSTRATIONS   108

ACKNOWLEDGEMENTS

This volume is a collection of essays that consists partly of the Baker Street Babes' contributions to our tumblr series Femme Friday, as well as essays written after we posted a call for contributions on our social media sites. We tried to include as many ladies as possible, though we are aware that we missed the likes of Mrs. Cushing from "The Cardboard Box," Nancy Barclay from "The Crooked Man," Emilia Lucca from "The Red Circle" as well as the ladies from "The Greek Interpreter" and "The Retired Colourman," and probably a few others. However, we have assembled quite the collection of essays on awesome ladies, so we beg forgiveness from the fantastic ladies we did not manage to include.

We want to thank those who took the time to write for us and who were patient throughout the long process of getting this book together. Since we had several enthusiastic replies requesting to write about the same ladies and we picked writers on a first come first serve basis. However, we would like to thank every single one of you who offered to write something! Your enthusiasm and helpfulness mean a lot to us.

Thank you also to those who commented on our posts and engaged in conversation with us about this project.

Further thanks go out to Lyndsay Faye, who birthed this project, and who is one of the most amazing women I know. Furthermore, to every single one of the Baker Street Babes, both current and past members, who are all amazing and strong ladies, who sacrifice a lot of time, resources and energy in order to share our mutual love for Sherlock Holmes and his world with our readership and audience. I am also truly grateful to Merilyn Paugus for her gracious offer to let us use her amazing art in this volume.

Last but not least, I would like to thank the kind and brilliant Sherlockians who have supported and continue to support us, our projects and our feminist points of view.

Maria Fleischhack

INTRODUCTION

Femme Fridays came about, as so many of life's best and most eccentric ideas come about, thanks at least in part to adversity.

Literary social clubs, fandoms, and all similar conclaves of enthusiasts are prone to upheaval from time to time, and the world of Sherlockiana is no exception. A thriving, passionate, and diverse group of Holmes lovers spanning many nations and seven separate continents, we are open and witty, dry and caring, affectionate and critical. On an average day, we brighten the spirits with a toast or a tweet, and at our best, we throw wide our doors and make our very homes the home of any professed follower of the Great Detective and the Good Doctor who happens to be in need. If you're holding this book, you're very probably one of us, and we salute you – there isn't a finer or more generous gang of misfits on the planet.

When Femme Friday was conceived, however, there were stirrings of discontentment stemming from several widely varied sources. Rare but distressing events paralleling the "fake geek girl" controversy in the wider culture of fannish validity had forced some young female Sherlockians to defend their seats at the established table. The decidedly non-villainous character of Irene Adler, beloved by practically our entire population, in Guy Ritchie's otherwise rippingly droll films for Warner Brothers, was first relegated to playing the role of Professor Moriarty's FedEx service and then left for dead on the floor of a restaurant. And how can we forget the woman Watson loved, that "lighthouse" to the troubled, Mary Morstan, shooting a certain titular hero in the chest in the wildly popular BBC adaptation?

The Baker Street Babes were dismayed over the increasing negativity but certainly not daunted by it. What can we do? became the battle cry. How best to exhort and affirm our sisters? And so, as social media has always been a favorite medium of ours when reaching out to our comrades from New York to New Delhi, we took to tumblr with a fresh weekly theme: unabashed praise of the many mighty women of the Sherlock Holmes universe. Wives and widows. The sung and the unsung. Victorian adventuresses and modern day Yard officers. The noblest of bluebloods and the destitute little girls who doubtlessly formed a percentage of the Baker Street Irregulars. In short, any female character we could think of who kicked ass, took names, or wished a saucy good-night to Mr. Sherlock Holmes.

Femme Friday caught on quickly, mainly, I believe, because the Babes had so much fun lauding our favorite ladies. We were downright giddy with it. At first, we threw our virtual parades for classic characters from the Sir Arthur Conan Doyle adventures, but soon enough we were extolling the virtues of Molly the lab technician and Olivia the mouse. The mission was unique in the sense that we were all writing in very much our own styles, from easy breezy to scholarly assurance, without the inkling that the project would ever be compiled into a complete volume. It was simply a way of putting pure feminist optimism on the internet, when so much of that particular engine is so often devoted to … well, to not pure feminist optimism. To hell with this, we decided. Give us a thoughtfully explicated ode to a female instead of the 140-character ravings of a Twitter troll any day.

The results, I am proud to say, are before you. Every essay in this anthology was written about a woman, by a woman, and was edited by women and published by the Babes. But this lovingly chronicled virtual movement is by no means for women exclusively. It's for every Sherlockian who has ever raised a pint with one of us, chatted online with us, or picked up a copy of the canon and at some point thought, "what a woman!"

In other words, absolutely everybody. May the next enterprise in the cause of pure feminist optimism prove half as much fun.

Lyndsay Faye

THE LADIES

Irene Adler
by Lyndsay Faye

Irene Adler means many things to many people. For some, she is the first truly legendary antagonist faced by Sherlock Holmes. (Because really … do you spend much time ruminating over errant Mormons? Does Jonathan Small get your panties in a twist?)

For others, she is a plucky ringlet-haired sass machine who is allowed to tweak Robert Downey Jr. by the nose, or a naked she-dervish who spanks her way to fame and fortune only to have it (questionably, maybe even egregiously) plucked away from her. For still others, she is a mere mask worn by that murderous maven Jaime Moriarty, whose half-smile never fails to break the brain of anyone who dares to look at Natalie Dormer without protective eyewear.

But who is Irene Adler, really? Or at least…who *was* she originally? And why do we love her so?

It would be ridiculous to say that we love Irene Adler because "To Sherlock Holmes, she is always *the* woman," because pleeeeeeeze. Is this fact canonically true and completely awesome? Yes, indeed. Is it a bit of Watsonian ridiculousness? Thank you for asking, because this fella was not exactly the *Encyclopedia Brittanica* of narrators, and we have as much real evidence that Holmes gazed longingly at Irene's printed selfie as we have that he was gently tipped off a cliff by an elderly academic with head-oscillation issues. Irene appears in one case. (As does Moriarty.) She is mentioned in another. (As is Moriarty.) But both remain iconic figures in the Sherlock Holmes canon, and I would posit that this is the reason: they absolutely defy our expectations of them, and they redefine Holmes's world in doing so. They make him capable of *failure*. And in both cases, he respects them for it wholeheartedly.

Sherlock Holmes is a ninja and a boxer and a singlestick fighter and a hottie and a genius and an artist, and we adore him, but he needs to be put in his place from time to time. In the *very first short story in which Holmes appears*, and I cannot emphasize this enough, he gets his ivory ass kicked by a girl wearing trousers. And lest we forget, this story was written by a white dude whose colonialist mores wouldn't ever have been questioned by any of his peers – Sir Arthur Conan Doyle was a gentleman and a scholar and a divorce reform advocate, no question. But he was hardly a revolutionary, and he still decided that his chosen protagonist's first short format case would be a gleeful schooling by a woman in a questionable profession who owns her autonomy, mops the playing field with the King of Bohemia, and ultimately gets the groom and whisks Godfrey Norton off on her muscled white charger.

Why is this good storytelling, and what do we take away from Adler as a result? First, Irene Adler exists fully as a completely separate entity from Holmes and Watson, one who is capable of besting them. When she wins the day, we understand that Holmes gambles from time to time, takes risks and loses his wagers, and this allows narrative tension to exist even though his skills are almost superhuman. If we were to look at Holmes as a statistical bet and think he's unstoppable, what would be the point in reading the story? Defeating him makes readers crave more dramatic tension, and Doyle was a genius to realize this. Second, unlike many characters who represent either a Problem to Be Solved or a Victim to Be Saved or a Threat to Be Thwarted, Adler simply

has plans that do not coincide with those of the great detective or the good doctor. She isn't a menace to them and she isn't a boon either. She's a person.

Adler is simply trying to live her life on her terms and take a hot lawyer to bed when she feels like it, and the greatest thing about this is that Doyle ultimately says AW YISS and

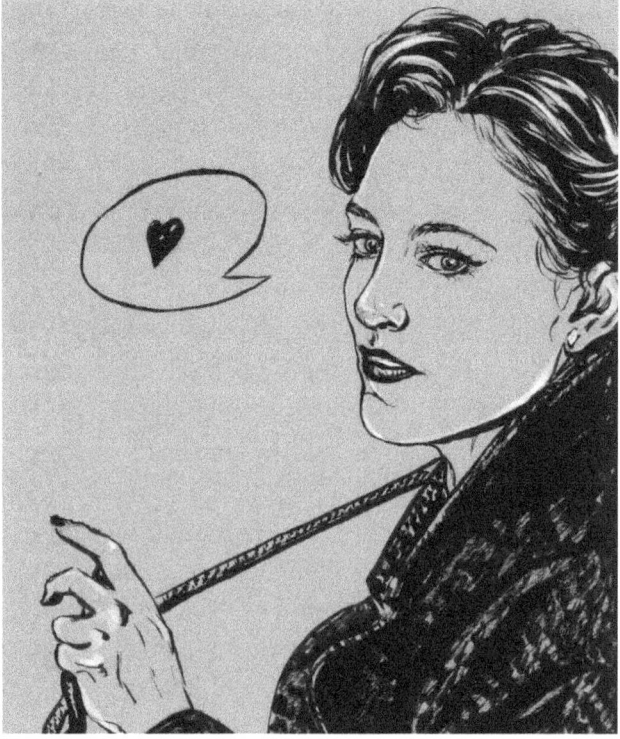

3

lets her get away with …

… were you filling in the blank with murder?

And here is an interesting point: the Irene Adler of the canon is one true Lady Gaga-style free bitch, and she is cast as the antagonist, but she never stoops to any measures other than retaining a photograph *which belongs to her, presumably,* and … cross-dressing? (Do you have to stoop to cross-dress? You have to stoop to pull trousers on, but … never mind.)

It's interesting that modern adaptations have chosen to make Adler either 1) complicit with the archvillain Moriarty, or 2) ACTUALLY the archvillain Moriarty. Rachel McAdams is fabulously coy but acts nevertheless as his postal service. Lara Pulver is delectably brilliant but hires him to learn how to "play the Holmes brothers." And Natalie Dormer … well … *cough.* All nods to her strength of character and her feminism. But surely we ought to question why nowadays Irene must be a villain in order to exist in a narrative.

So while we love all of these Irene Adlers for their resourcefulness, their fearlessness, and their charm, let us never forget to raise a glass to the canonical Adventuress as well: the Woman, who proved that you don't have to be either a villain or a damsel in order to win the day.

Irene Adler is one of the most famous characters in all the Sherlock Holmes canon. She eclipses and predominates the whole of her sex, and every single incarnation of her has been a fascinating delight, even when squirrelly bits worm their way in. And for your wisdom and your love of high adventure, Ms. Adler, we salute you – no less than for your general cheekiness, and your capacity to put even Sherlock Holmes in his place.

Maud Bellamy
by Fabienne Courouge

First of all, I'd like to share the reaction I had when I read "The Adventure of the Lion's Mane" many years ago. I found myself quite perplexed by the oddity of the story and the gap between what I read and the image I had forged of the consulting detective. For several years, I disregarded this adventure, a bump in the canonical road …

Bewilderingly, in this tale, the man "who loathed every form of society with his whole Bohemian soul" became "friendly [with Stackhurst] from the day [he] came to the coast, and [they] could drop in on each other in the evenings without an invitation."

Even worse: Holmes confesses he sometimes enjoys a swim in company of McPherson (can you just imagine the scene? Can you imagine Sherlock Holmes wading into shallow waves in a 1900's swimsuit?): "Summer and winter he went for his swim, and, as I am a swimmer myself, I have often joined him."

I'm not the first one to point out how different from Watson's usual portrayal of Holmes's personality this narrative appears, so I won't go into further detail. But "The Adventure of the Lion Mane" is written in the first person narrative voice, so let's suspend disbelief, and let's consider that the tale offers a more intimate glimpse of a Sherlock Holmes, who, on this occasion only (with the exception of "The Blanched Soldier"), decides to share directly with his readers something about his more human side. And Maud belongs to this side.

"I will be there, you may be sure": Maud Bellamy is revealed to the reader through this sentence, written on a note found in the victim's pocket. "I will be there, you may be sure," I dare say, is a sentence that can be applied to Maud Bellamy in many way, in spite of her brief appearance in the tale and her minor role in the plot.

She'll be there, on each list of outstanding women of the canon. She'll be there, among the beautiful women, indubitably. Although Holmes is warned that "[e]veryone knows her. She is the beauty of the neighborhood - a real beauty, [...] who would draw attention everywhere," the detective can't help but be distracted when he comes to meet her.

"I could not look upon her perfect clear-cut face, with all the soft freshness of the downlands in her delicate coloring, without realizing that no young man would cross her path unscathed." Such were Holmes's thoughts, occurring in the middle of a reasoning process. What did Miss Bellamy do to the "most perfect reasoning and observing machine who never spoke of the softer passions, save with a gibe and a sneer?"

She'll be there, among the strong women, definitely: Holmes is impressed by her "composed concentration which showed [him] that she possessed strong character as well as great beauty." Indeed, the reader can easily figure out how Maud, raised motherless in undistinguished surrounding, daughter of an oaf, sister of a lout (Edward F Clark, "Maud Bellamy" in: *BSJ* No. 29, p. 70) grew, amazingly, into a "rare a flower from such a root and in such an atmosphere" and shaped her strong inner personality on her own.

No wonder she didn't hesitate to stand up against everyone to protect her engagement to McPherson and overruled her family by steadily offering Holmes sympathy and help ("If I can help to show who did it, it is the least I can do for him who is gone"). Holmes qualifies her as the one who "will always remain in [his] memory as a most complete and remarkable woman." And let's remember that he has met quite a few remarkable women in his time: Violet Hunter may be "exceptional," Mary Morstan may have a "decided genius," and Irene Adler may "eclipse and predominate the whole of her sex." And yet, Maud Bellamy still seems to lead the list.

Therefore, a number of Sherlockians have classified Maud Bellamy as Holmes's true love. Brad Keefauver of Sherlock Peoria wrote: "Forget Mary Russell and Irene Adler. Maud Bellamy! The one woman we have Sherlock Holmes's direct testimony on" (http://sherlockpeoria.blogspot.fr/2014/07/summer-of-sherlock-lions-mane.html). Julia Rosenblatt, BSI, has even proposed that Holmes loved and married Maud once her mourning period was over (Leslie S Klinger, *The New Annotated Sherlock Holmes: The Complete Short Stories*, p. 1677).

Would I go that far? I don't think so (I like my detectives wild, free and lonely) and sticking to the text, there's no real evidence that Holmes fell for Maud. The story takes place in 1907, so, considering the generally admitted date of 1854 as Holmes's birth year, he's 53 when he meets Maud, who is in her early twenties. Would we imagine Holmes succumbing to middle-age lust? In any case, he doesn't express a personal liking, but a deep comprehension of her attractiveness.

But maybe she stirred something in Holmes; maybe a hint of regret of what could have been if "all emotions [had not been] abhorrent to his cold, precise but admirably balanced mind." I'll illustrate this last conjecture with this beautiful dialogue about Maud from Bert Coules's radio drama:

Holmes: "Women have seldom been an attraction for me ..."

Watson: "Seldom? Are you saying she was an exception?"

Holmes (quickly and defensively): "Certainly not."

Watson: "Holmes, you're supposed to be giving me data, remember? What was she like?"

Holmes: "She would have graced any assembly in the world, Watson. Perfect, clear-cut face, delicate colouring of the downlands in her cheeks, such poise and control ..."

[pause]

Holmes: "Watson ... I have devoted my life to investigating the dark side of humanity. What have I missed ...?"

Watson (with a sigh): "There's no way to tell."

Holmes: "No ... logical way, perhaps."

(BBC Radio, "The Lion's Mane," dramatised by Bert Coules, produced and directed by Patrick Rayner, broadcast on 8th March 1995)

Mary Brackenstall
by Ashley D. Polasek

Sir Arthur Conan Doyle was not always a man of progressive ideals: he was anti-suffragist and pro-imperialist, a British gentleman of traditional sensibilities in many ways. That's one reason why Lady Mary Brackenstall is one of his most intriguing female characters. The story in which she figures – "The Adventure of the Abbey Grange" – is a treatise on the need for divorce law reform, and Lady Mary is a symbol of the ultimate triumph of a victim over her abuser. Basically, she's a stone-cold badass.

"Abbey Grange" was published in 1904, and follows Holmes and Watson as they attempt to solve the murder of Sir Eustace Brackenstall, who had his head smashed in "like a rotten pumpkin" (there's some imagery for you) at his home in Kent. The case is nearly over before it begins; by the time Holmes and Watson arrive at Abbey Grange, Brackenstall's wife, who witnessed the murder, has regained her composure and given a full account which, according to Holmes, "is corroborated by every detail we see before us." A remarkable statement, considering the whole thing, as Holmes later discovers, is a complete fabrication.

Thus we begin to appreciate Lady Mary: bold enough to lie to Holmes's face, calm enough to pass it off without question, and clever enough to convince England's leading mind that he should trust her words over his observations. (He noticed, after all, the key clue directly, but talked himself out of it because his instincts contradicted Mary's tale.)

Holmes himself later tells Watson that "[t]he lady's charming personality must not be permitted to warp our judgment." Wait, was Holmes allowing his judgment to be warped by a GIRL? This must be some woman! How charming is she? The expert in these matters is always Three Continents Watson, so let's see: "Graceful," "womanly," "beautiful," "blonde," "golden-haired," "blue-eyed," "perfect complexion," and let's not leave out her "quick, observant gaze" and "alert expression." Watson doesn't miss a trick.

The subtext of the story is even more illuminating when it comes to Lady Mary's character. When we meet her after her husband's death in early 1897, she has only been in England for 18 months. Originally from

Adelaide, Australia, Lady Mary left her home with only her trusted maid in tow, and, as far as we can tell, no immediate prospects awaiting her. It would be fair, therefore, to brand her an adventuress, and, true to form, she attracts men like a bacon-wrapped stripper. She is married to a wealthy baronet within six months, leaving a trail of broken hearts behind her.

None of this is what is most remarkable about Lady Mary, however. Her most remarkable quality is her will to survive in the face of physical, verbal, and deep psychological abuse. Her husband was a drunkard and a villain. Not only did he punch her in the face and stab her with a hatpin (seriously? WTF?), he threw a decanter at her maid, called her "the vilest name that a man could use to a woman" (we can only guess), and poured petroleum on her dog and *set it on fire*. When all of this comes to light during the investigation, she does not cower and she is not ashamed. Instead, she eloquently declares that "[i]t is a sacrilege, a crime, a villainy to hold that such a marriage is binding. I say that these monstrous laws of [England] will bring a curse upon the land – God will not let such wickedness endure."

With this, Lady Mary Brackenstall establishes herself as a testament to the perseverance of high spirit and true beauty in the face of injustice. We are given more hope and closure than we often get for the victims of these tales, as the killer – Captain Jack "fine specimen of manhood" Crocker is absolved by Holmes and Watson, and invited to return in a year's time to make his suit to Lady Mary. We can only infer that this picture of wit and grace has not only survived her ordeal but, to cap her victory, pocketed a sexy sailor who appreciates her for the wickedly fierce woman she is. Carry on, Lady Mary.

Lady Frances Carfax
by Emma Schlimgen

Dazzling deductions, brilliant disguises, and a race against time are what you will find in "The Disappearance of Lady Frances Carfax." These features can present themselves in any number of stories in the *Sherlock Holmes* canon. What makes this one particularly spectacular is the missing lady herself. From her kind-hearted disposition to her extravagant lifestyle as a bachelorette, she manages to remind us of what we strive for in life. So now I straighten my deerstalker, turn up the BBC Big Band Orchestra, and dig into my *Complete Sherlock Holmes* to bring you just what makes this leading lady so special.

The first thing that catches my eye is Lady Carfax's dazzling description. Beneath the rather dismal account Holmes gives of her status as a "friendless woman," there is element of strength and determination that can resonate with many of us. Here, within the narrative, a picture is painted in our minds of a woman who is actually quite capable of providing for herself. Holmes remarks that "[s]he was left with limited means," yet she manages to have a maid, travel, and possess impressive articles of Spanish jewelry. Just from this account, I feel proud of this fictional Lady Carfax. She may not be the most sociable or particularly well-to-do woman, but she appears to be able to live life comfortably at her own standards and no one else's. We should all strive to do what is best for ourselves and not have to worry about our status or current situation, as Lady Carfax has so elegantly demonstrated.

The next interesting aspect concerning our lady in question is her reputation as someone who displays an immense kindness. Holmes recounts how she writes to her governess every other week and has done so for the past four years. To me, this is extremely admirable and impressive. I correspond with my old instructors probably twice a year, and of course on social media. As someone who believes that letter correspondence needs to make a comeback, this little fact about Lady Carfax lightens my heart. I feel that it is important to look for that level of kindheartedness in ourselves. If we wrote letters for that long to *anyone*, it is sure to leave a remarkable impression. Lady Frances's maid and the manager of the Hotel National at Lausanne had both contributed to this notion, leaving the impression that her mistress was an extremely likable woman (and who wouldn't admire that?). One of the other most captivating pieces of Dr. Watson's narrative is how Lady Carfax left a man of a rather coarse personality so deeply in love with her. That, in my opinion, testifies to the fact that she was so enthralling, everyone felt some sort of love or respect for her. I believe that with our strength and kindness, we too could leave the same impression on those around us; something which I find important.

One further aspect that I feel I should touch on is the feeling towards this woman as presented by Dr. Watson and Mr. Sherlock Holmes (and by default, Sir Arthur Conan Doyle). Beyond the descriptions of her personality, her status, and her wealth, there seems to be another underlying tone of respect for her. Holmes calls her a "pathetic figure" and then three words later "a beautiful woman." It strikes me as strange that he would even acknowledge her beauty, but it also makes me appreciative that someone so stone cold could still recognize the attribute. Dr. Watson also demonstrates a harsh determination to save this woman from her demise. I tip my deerstalker to Sir Arthur for creating a female character of such inspiration, and one which his other characters (male and female) actually appreciate. With this recent rise of feminism and women in media, this is something quite surprising and refreshing to see from a story written in 1911. So, good on you, Sir Arthur!

Although she is quite fictional, this woman has reminded me of myself in some ways, and reminded me of what we should all strive to be. Whether it's her good nature, her self-sufficiency, her good name, or even her Spanish jewels, she sets an example of our strengths. These characteristics, as well as the attitude of her peers towards her, are something that we can apply to our own lives, no matter in which century.

Anna Coram
by Katie Magnusson

When I first read "The Golden Pince-Nez," I remember wondering why Anna Coram committed suicide. For such a strong woman, described by Watson as having "a certain nobility in the woman's bearing, a gallantry in the defiant chin and in the upraised head, which compelled something of respect and admiration," to ensure her death by taking poison, shortly before telling her tale, seems overly cinematic and unnecessarily dramatic. Holmes doesn't even make any sort of comment after the fact. A woman dies in front of him, and he merely ties up the loose ends of the case. It turns what seemed like it might have been an ending with some significance into something almost anticlimactic, for all its drama.

On the other hand, Anna's story would make a spectacular movie. The setting is 1870s Russia. The Nihilist movement, a counter-cultural philosophy rejecting all authorities, has shifted into a revolutionary force. Anna and Sergius, a young woman and her husband in the movement, are arrested by the authorities. The husband betrays not only his wife, but their friends, including one who was innocent, with no connections to the 'Brotherhood' at all. Anna is sent to Siberia, where she works in a prison camp for years, all the time knowing that her treacherous husband has escaped, and is living free, in a new life. She swears she will find him, and that she will free her friend, Alexis, whom Sergius had testified against, just to save his own skin.

At last, the opportunity comes; her sentence is fulfilled, and she is released. She tracks down her husband in England, where he has been living as a professor. She knows he has documents that would free Alexis. She finds out where he lives, discovers where the documents are kept, and prepares to steal them. Her theft is interrupted by the professor's secretary, and in her desperation to escape, theft turns into murder. Her glasses, a golden pince-nez, go missing in the struggle, and so she blindly makes her way down a passage she hopes will lead to safety, only to find herself in her hated husband's room. He agrees to shelter her, but only because it will protect himself as well. If she were to reveal his whereabouts to the Brotherhood, he'd turn her over to the authorities for murder. Neither of them expect the police to seek assistance from a particularly skilled consulting detective. Upon hearing her crime described in surprising detail, and having her secret hiding place revealed, Anna … takes poison, and dies. Perhaps they'd change the ending for the movie.

Of course, Holmes has already figured out how the crime occurred, and asserts multiple times that the murder was not intentional. Anna is confident enough in Holmes's honor and sense of justice to trust him with the documents that will free her friend, but clearly not enough to trust that he might be able to help her regarding Scotland Yard and a possible trial. Is death truly so much more desirable than an English jail cell? Did she fear being sent back to Russia so much?

We have to remember that this is a woman who has already seen immense hardship. The story says her husband has been in England for "some years." If we presume he went to England straight from Russia, it means multiple years for Anna to spend in a katorga, the precursor to the gulag of the Soviet Union. After years of forced labor and terrible living conditions, it would be easily understandable if Anna wanted revenge on her husband who had sent her there. Yet, she doesn't seek it. She says to him, "[…] it is not for me

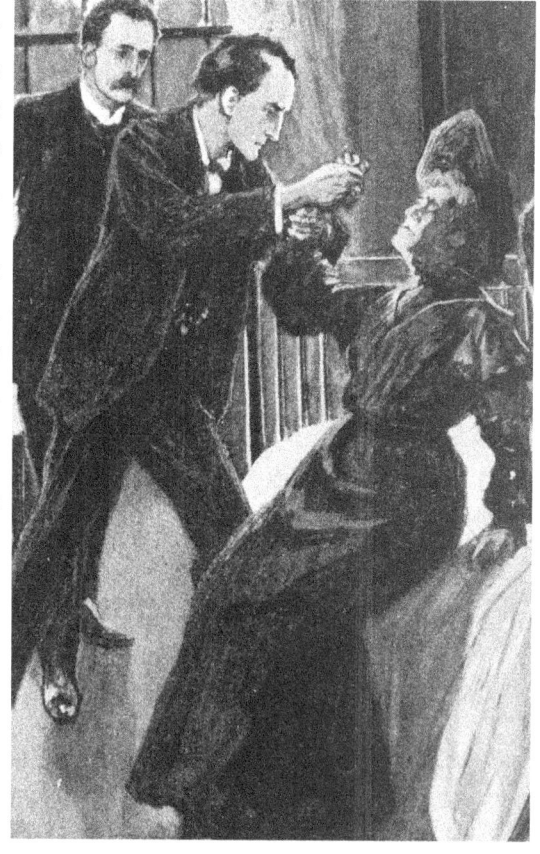

to cause the frail thread to be snapped before God's time [...]. Think of that, you villain, you villain; now, now, at this very moment, Alexis, a man whose name you are not worthy to speak, works and lives like a slave, and yet I have your life in my hands and I let you go."

What Anna wants is justice. She wants her friend free, and the truth known. This is her one goal in life. Perhaps, realizing her goal cannot be accomplished once she is trapped by her husband, and then the authorities, she decides to trust the honor of a stranger who might be able to fulfill her purpose. We don't know much about Anna Coram, but what we do know is that she is a noble woman who has had a difficult life, and who has seen the cause she fought for dissipate, and who has watched on helplessly as the people she cared about most were condemned to suffer.

Her last words are addressed to Holmes: "I charge you, sir, to remember the packet."

He does remember, and in taking it to the Russian embassy, he ensures that her death, an act of defiance against the life she endured, was not rendered meaningless.

As she handed that packet of documents to Sherlock Holmes, trusting his love of justice – a sentiment she saw reflected in herself – to see her mission completed, she completed the only thing she had left to live for. Her vial of poison must have been on her person the entire time. I think that the noble woman always knew her last act in life would be to die on her own terms.

That sentiment, at least, is perhaps worthy of the respect Anna compelled in Watson and his companions as she walked into the room from behind the bookcase.

Elsie Cubitt
by Tamar Zeffren

In "The Adventure of the Dancing Men," the reader never encounters Elsie Cubitt directly. Her actions and emotions are conveyed to the reader through various men: most importantly, her husband Hilton Cubitt; Sherlock Holmes, of course; and the villainous Abe Slaney.

When Hilton Cubitt appears before Sherlock Holmes at 221B Baker Street, he is described, warmly, as a "man of the old English soil – simple, straight, and gentle." The narrative works quite diligently to persuade us of Mr. Cubitt's honesty – and thus leads us to repose great trust in his estimation of his wife's integrity. When an honorable man describes his wife as, variously, "a truthful woman," "very straight," and as mindful of his family's honor as her own, such that "[s]he would never bring any stain upon it – of that I am sure," there emerges the impression of a stalwart and trustworthy woman.

When Sherlock presses his client to directly question his wife about the titular characters and their appearance on correspondence that makes Elsie Cubitt increasingly uneasy, Mr. Cubitt, endearingly, affirms his trust in his wife's integrity and demurs: "A promise is a promise, Mr. Holmes. If Elsie wished to tell me she would. If not, it is not for me to force her confidence. But I am justified in taking my own line – and I will."

Elsie Cubitt basks in reflected glory, both that of her husband's praise of her and of the high estimation in which the narrator holds her husband. Hilton Cubitt praises Elsie – but she is worthy of praise because she is a helpmeet worthy of him.

These conclusions about Elsie's character are, somewhat ironically, echoed by the story's villain. Abe Slaney, an associate – and fellow criminal – of Elsie's father in Chicago. Slaney was engaged to Elsie. However, "she couldn't stand the business, and she had a bit of honest money of her own, so she gave us all the slip and got away to London," where she eventually meets and marries Hilton Cubitt, and moves with him to Norfolk. Slaney dogs Elsie across the Atlantic, and starts sending her encoded messages at her husband's estate.

Abe Slaney's sordid account further affirms that Elsie is a

determined and resilient woman, equally desperate to escape past associations and to prevent any shadow on her husband's honor. The only letter she sends Abe Slaney, he reports, "implore[d] me to go away, and saying that it would break her heart if any scandal should come upon her husband."

Though unfortunately Elsie emerges from these tragic events a widow, her sterling qualities of loyalty and integrity indeed have the last word. At the story's conclusion, Watson reports that, in fitting tribute to her well-matched partner, the resilient Elsie Cubitt "remains a widow, devoting her whole life to the care of the poor and to the administration of her husband's estate."

Sally Donovan
by Amy Thomas

Sherlock Holmes is a polarizing figure, no matter when or where he appears. Some, like John Watson and Mrs. Hudson, learn to accept and even love Sherlock for his brilliance and eccentricity, and in spite of his frequent coldness and lack of expressed emotional sensitivity. Others, found in every incarnation of Holmes's world, dislike and oppose him, arguably a more normal and expected response to some of his behavior. These characters are not villains or heroes on a grand scale. They are Sherlock's everyday irritants, the wrenches in the works of The Game. One such character is Sergeant Sally Donovan of Scotland Yard, a skilled, cynical police officer with a personal vendetta against her boss's favorite secret weapon. The following sections will evaluate her character in detail.

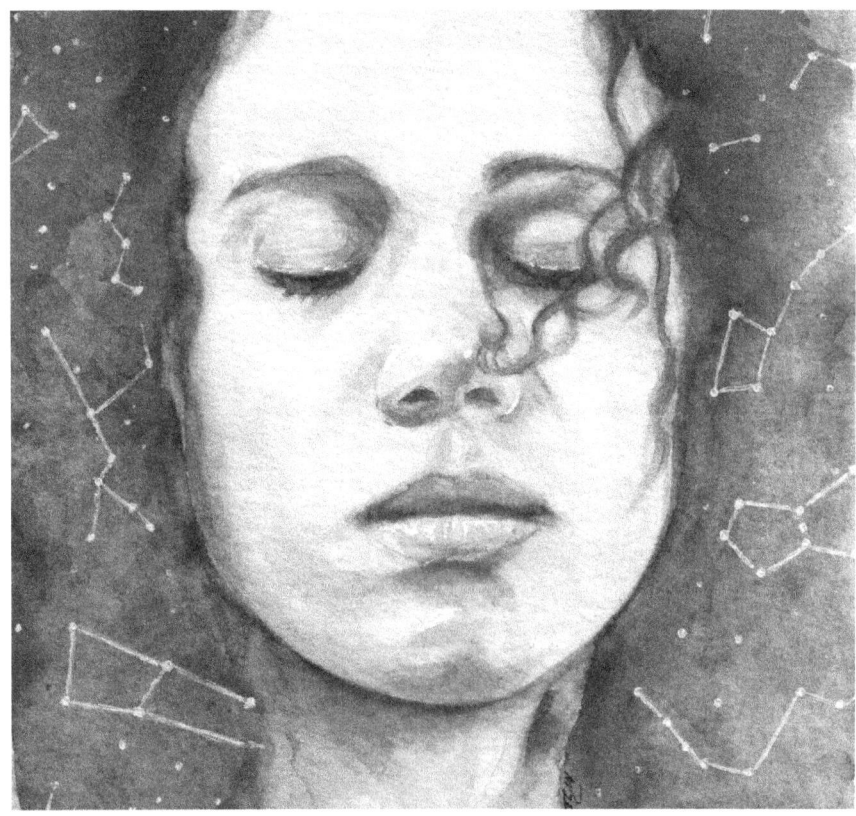

Sally is one of the very first characters introduced in A *Study in Pink*, and she appears in her professional capacity as Inspector Lestrade of Scotland Yard's right-hand officer. The immediate implications are clear: Sally is almost certainly skilled, intelligent, and upwardly mobile, or she would not have reached her position at her age. Her frustration with Sherlock Holmes is also made clear very quickly because of her negative reaction to his text-message disruptions of Scotland Yard's press conference. Lestrade is bemused, but Sally is angry, a difference that carries throughout the series.

As the story continues, Sherlock shows Sally and forensic specialist Anderson an uncharacteristic level of animosity when they oppose his work at the Lauriston Gardens crime scene. Sherlock is dismissive of most people, but he takes the time to verbalize his deductions about the affair between Sally and Anderson and is obviously aware of the discomfort it causes them. Anderson's embarrassment is apparent, and he seems to know that he cannot compete with Sherlock's mind, so he seethes internally. Sally, on the other hand, seems resigned to Sherlock's barbs, angry, but also cynical, as if she expects nothing else from him. The dynamics of this encounter are worth noting because they indicate a negative prior history between the characters.

Sally acts out her dislike for Sherlock when she becomes part of the drug bust Lestrade uses to blackmail him in A *Study in Pink*. She forms part of the group Lestrade wryly calls "very keen" to implicate Sherlock in illegal activities. Again, a contrast can be seen between her overt distaste for Sherlock and Lestrade's more cordial feelings. For Sally, the bust is clearly an attempt to get back at Sherlock for everything she hates about him. For Lestrade, it is a tool to nudge cooperation from an asset he admires but cannot figure out how to motivate.

Through A *Study in Pink* and *The Great Game*, Sally turns most of her attention to John Watson and tries to dissuade him from trusting or forming a close friendship with Sherlock. She tells him that Sherlock "gets off on" murder and calls him a psychopath who will someday be responsible for a murder himself. Later, as she sees John's involvement increasing, she again tries to convince him to abandon the relationship. Her motives for her repeated warnings seem mixed and are not completely clear. Perhaps she wants to hurt Sherlock by ruining his one real friendship; perhaps she feels some genuine concern for John; perhaps she sees herself in John and wants to spare him the angry disillusionment with Sherlock she herself seems to have experienced in the past. Whatever her full motivations, Sally acts as a constant, unavoidable antagonist in Sherlock's life, a woman who is unwilling to be impressed with his abilities no matter how impressive they are shown to be, and who opposes him personally and professionally as much as possible, even to the point of trying to drive a wedge between him and his flatmate.

In series two, Sally's antagonist role is solidified even further, as she turns dislike into outright opposition. When Sherlock's arc reaches its crescendo, she seems delighted to see him get what she thinks is his comeuppance. Still, considering her character perspective, her behavior is entirely consistent. If she were to suddenly flip positions in *The Reichenbach Fall*, it wouldn't make sense, and from her perspective, a man she has never trusted is finally being exposed as the fraud and criminal he is. It may not be a comfortable viewpoint for fans of Holmes, but it's certainly fitting for her.

Disappointing for fans of Sally and the amazing Vinette Robinson, her role was drastically limited in series three, but oh what a cameo it was. In a sequence very reminiscent of Doyle's "Redheaded League", Sally is finally shown to be the skilled, brave, and professional officer she's always been. While the fallout of the Holmes debacle has destroyed former antagonist Anderson's job and life, it hasn't been able to shake Sally. Instead, she's just as successful and forward-moving as ever. In a show called *Sherlock*, this is a bold move. It reminds the viewer that loving Sherlock Holmes isn't the only measure of a person's, or woman's, worth. Not by any means. Sally can go on distrusting Holmes until the cows come home, and she's still going to be one amazing police officer and gutsy woman.

Finally, series four was missing Sally altogether, though the showrunners said that they had envisioned character progression in which she no longer hated Sherlock. For fans, that would have been an interesting reconciliation to witness and could be seen in future series. Sherlock needs the presence of capable women like Sergeant Donovan, who advance in life without needing the affirmation or guidance of Holmes and Watson.

Meaning of the Role

Fans of the BBC's *Sherlock* find themselves divided in their opinions of Sally, with some liking and admiring her character's unwillingness to accept Sherlock's rudeness and others deploring her inability to see his brilliance. Either way, Sally is an inescapable part of the series and serves several purposes. This section will look at her character in three ways: Sally as a composite, Sally as a contrast, and Sally as a window into Sherlock.

First, Sally serves as a composite of several Holmes canon characters. Many different stories feature minor antagonists to Sherlock, unconvinced law enforcement officers and others who dislike his methods and do not believe in his brilliance. At times, Inspector Lestrade is one of these. The creators of Sherlock chose to focus on a different side of Lestrade, the more supportive and paternal side that leads him to become Sherlock's ally and even, at times, to act as his friend. As a result, they were left with an opening in an area that is almost always filled in Conan Doyle's stories, the role of the irritant who should be on Sherlock's side but chooses to oppose him instead. Rather than inventing a series of forgettable characters to fill this position, the Sherlock team chose to create Sally, a recurring character with an unexplained history of antagonism toward Sherlock and an insatiable appetite for insulting him. Sally may not be a popular character, but she is a strong and believable update of a canon concept.

Second, Sally serves as an accessible contrast between the world's conventional view of Sherlock and John's unrelenting friendship. Theoretically, from observing Sherlock's behavior, viewers can easily surmise that he would be likely to engender dislike in a great number of people. Sally is a specific example of how virulent this dislike can be, and her responses are not difficult to understand. The idea that Sally has formed a low opinion of a man who is constantly rude, abrupt, and arrogant is logical and believable. This is why her behavior provides a wonderful counterpoint to John's. In the face of extremely eccentric and sometimes sociopathic behavior, John is the anti-Sally, the friend who continues to care for Sherlock no matter what the world thinks. Having Sally as a physical example of the opposite view makes John's behavior seem all the more poignant.

Finally, Sally provides a window into Sherlock himself through the responses she provokes from him. As referenced above, Sherlock's response to most people is to dismiss them without a great deal of thought. In Sally's case, however, he behaves with actual antagonism in response to hers. His behavior can be interpreted in several ways, but some of his reactions seem to be the results of genuine pain. As he tells John early in the series, most people cannot stand him because of the knowledge his deductive abilities give him about them. Bank employee Sebastian bears this out in *The Blind Banker* when he says that none of Sherlock's university classmates liked him. Sally's treatment of Sherlock is an extension of the dislike that has followed him all of his life. Instead of coldly shrugging off her antagonism, Sherlock seems to feel the need to defend himself, proving that he capable of being hurt. Without Sally, this dimension of Sherlock's humanness would be less apparent.

Grace Dunbar
by Kristina "Curly" Manente

The scene is set: Mr. J. Neil Gibson, a former United States Senator, calls upon Sherlock Holmes. His wife is dead; shot in the head. Miss Grace Dunbar, their governess, is being held on suspicion of murder. But all is not as it seems.

It's a set up for any regular mystery, and truth be told, this mystery plays out without too many bells and whistles. In fact, the reader may have been able to parse this one together without Sherlock Holmes's help. "The Problem of Thor Bridge" is, in essence, a story of the wrongfully accused and perhaps the birth of the suicide-masked-as-murder trope.

Essentially what we have here is a governess, Grace, who is envied and

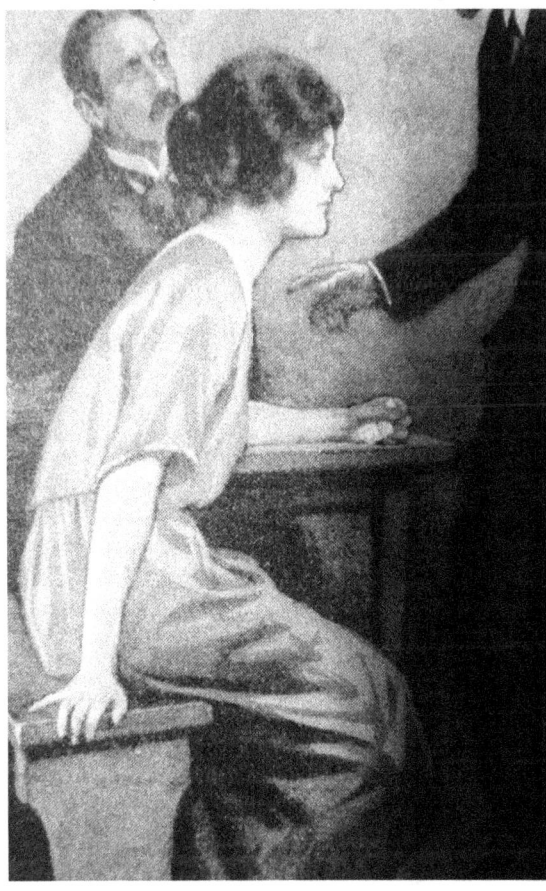

hated by Mrs. Gibson because her husband, who is cruel and unloving to her, has the hots for Grace, who doesn't want the lecherous dude feeling her up. It's a soap opera indeed, because it ends in murder. Or suicide, rather. Mrs. Gibson cleverly frames Grace by making her suicide on Thor Bridge, where she appointed the governess to meet her to essentially bitch her out, look like a murder. She shoots herself after Grace leaves, the gun disappearing thanks to being tied to a rock hanging over the bridge, drowning the evidence. She previously had deposited the twin firearm in Grace's room, making sure it had been recently fired, this way she would be implicated. And she is. And perhaps Mrs. Gibson would have gotten away with it, had it not been for the pesky Sherlock Holmes. Even though he's a bit slow on the uptake for this one.

"I have been sluggish in mind and wanting in that mixture of imagination and reality, which is the basis of my art." You and me both buddy.

Grace Dunbar did not commit murder. She did not commit adultery. In fact she did nothing wrong. Poor girl. What's important to note is that Grace Dunbar was exonerated. She didn't leave the employ of the Gibsons despite understanding Mr. Gibson's affection for her, but I have difficulty blaming her for that. She did not reciprocate the feelings, nor is she responsible for Mr. Gibson's. Mrs. Gibson's hatred of her comes from her husband's poor treatment for her; her grief and jealousy are what emboldens her to try and frame Grace for murder. It is not Grace's fault, though it is portrayed to be. Not many have written about Grace Dunbar. She's listed as just "another Violet," as boring and simply a plot device. It could be argued that Mr. Gibson petitions more for her innocence than Grace does herself, but one must remember his less than honorable intentions towards her. Of course he would try to have her released; he would feel she owed him her life then and who knows what he could have done then. It's already well established that he is a cruel man, especially to his late wife. Holmes does not take on the case because Gibson asks him too, he does it for the intrigue, and one would hope, to prove Grace innocent and let her get on with her life away from Gibson's wandering eyes.

As such, might it be put forward that the strength in the character of Grace Dunbar is her patience and quiet determination? Her determination to prove herself innocent, even if in a demure way. She is honest and forthright, she doesn't make a spectacle of herself, and she assists Holmes in the investigation by being a great suspect in explaining herself. She does not doubt herself. Is this not indication that she is a woman deserving of our respect? She is framed for the most heinous of crimes, yet she does not succumb to it.

The fact is, she did not commit murder. Not only is this the key point that Holmes takes up this case for, but it is also important in a personal context.

I have a vested interest in Grace Dunbar, because she is my investiture name for The Baker Street Irregulars. I realized after the word "exonerated" that it was me being spoken of, as did most of the people around me. To finally be proven not to be the 'fake Sherlockian' that I had been marred as by certain corners of the Sherlockian worlds, I was granted what many may see as the highest honor.

This is nothing like being cleared for murder, to be fair, but it has enough parallels with my own story that I do find my investiture rather apt. Though please, no one frame me for murder.

I like to think that Grace went on to work as a governess with a nicer family, one without wretched husbands, crazy wives, and far less suicide. One can only hope.

Mrs. Ferguson
by Evadare Volney

Ladies of the canon who originate from points other than familiar old England (or at least respectable outposts of the British Empire) bring baggage with them, and Mrs. Ferguson of "The Adventure of the Sussex Vampire" is no exception. One thing she does not bring with her to the story is her original name - we know her only as wife and mother subsumed into the fold of her husband's good name. Part of her baggage - her maid, Dolores - gets a name that suggests independence, which isn't really much of a courtesy in this case.

This might be fitting, because what sets Mrs. Ferguson apart turns out to be her phenomenal loyalty and devotion to her role, though she emotes in a manner that's not exactly to the manor born. We first meet her indirectly through a letter by someone who is claiming NOT to be Mr Robert Ferguson, who is babbling in print about vampires. Watson is already feeling a little bit testy with his friend Holmes. "It was one of the peculiarities of his proud, self-contained nature that though he docketed any fresh information very quietly and accurately in his brain, he seldom made any acknowledgement to the giver." But Watson warms to the chase, as always when the aid-seeker turns out to be a legitimate old acquaintance of his.

It is through this letter that we first meet Mrs. Ferguson, through the words of someone trying to seem much more impartial than he is:

This gentleman married some five years ago a Peruvian lady, the daughter of a Peruvian merchant, whom he had met in connection with the importation of nitrates. The lady was very beautiful, but the fact of her foreign birth and her alien religion always caused a separation of interests and of feelings between husband and wife, so that after a time his love may have cooled towards her and he may have come to regard their union as a mistake. He felt there were sides of her character which he could never explore or understand. This was the more painful as she was as loving a wife as a man could have — to all appearance absolutely devoted.

Then again, one doesn't have to be terribly exotic to get this treatment either: recall Rachel Howell, the heartbreak-maddened murderess of "The Musgrave Ritual", who "was of Welsh blood, fiery and passionate."

"Foreign birth" and "alien religion" (presumably Catholicism since actual "alien" religions like Scientology and Cthulhu-worship weren't invented yet) are exotifying terms, and the few Latinas who made their way to the England of canon generally get this treatment. Compare the Peruvian Mrs. Ferguson, for example, to the Brazilian Mrs. Gibson of "Thor Bridge" (nee Maria Pinto) who is described in lush and unrepentant terms: "passionate, whole-hearted, tropical, ill-balanced." Mrs. Gibson has the misfortune of passionately loving a fickle husband who cools to her and becomes cruel as soon as the "romance" has passed. Rather than fade politely into the background as a no-longer-loved wife ought to in a wealthy man's world, Mrs. Gibson becomes a schemer who commits suicide and frames her rival for murder at the same time. Mrs. Ferguson at least appears to have chosen a better man, or to have been chosen by a better one: Mr. Ferguson might be a bit of a dolt, but nowhere near such a nasty piece of work as Mr. Gibson.

And, more importantly to the Victorian imagination, Mrs. Ferguson's love for her child forces her to creative and resourceful, if rather melodramatic means to save her baby from the imminent threat. The threat, after all, is one that she is in a unique position to recognize. Like Mrs. Grant Munro, aka Effie Hebron, in "The Yellow Face", the reason she must deceive her husband is a bit of baggage from the homeland, repurposed in gruesome manner here at home by the adorable little psychopath Jacky.

But Mrs. Ferguson's theatrical, melodramatic stubbornness in keeping the truth from her husband is even more ridiculously selfless than Mrs. Munro's motive (fearing rejection by her husband if he'd known her late first husband was black, as is her still-living child) – Mrs. Ferguson just wants to spare her husband the heartbreak of knowing that one of his beloved children has tried to kill the other, even if she couldn't quite restrain herself from smacking the would-be murderer around a little bit herself. Foreign women, after all. So hot-blooded.

She attempts to preserve her husband's feelings in the most theatrical manner possible – by taking to her bed and refusing to see him. A reader doesn't have to be as perceptive as Sherlock Holmes to suspect that she sets up an unsustainable crisis situation so that eventually the truth must come out. Her maid, strong-willed Dolores with the painfully-written accent, must run interference between husband and wife while the baby stays under guard. Mr. Ferguson is clearly a spectacular idiot, for at least three women in the household know the secret of the dog's mysterious ailment and of the real reason why Mrs. Ferguson was seen sucking blood from her baby's neck, and why all the South American poison darts have gone missing – and decided this was information he could not be trusted with.

Once having admitted Watson to her presence, Mrs. Ferguson puts on a stage worthy performance: despair, dementia, delirium, and supernatural delusions of devils and fiends – and anger at her husband, whom she thinks really ought to trust her when it comes to the safety of "a very beautiful child, dark-eyed, golden-haired, a wonderful mixture of the Saxon and the Latin."

Between the lines of Mrs. Ferguson's theatrical retreat and performative refusals, and Dolores's nearly as potent performance ("I fear she die") is written a sad but cunning truth: Mrs. Ferguson was glad to see Dr. Watson, and by extension have her story told by Holmes, because Mr. Ferguson was going to need to hear the truth from the mouth of a white English mansplainer, or else he could not hear it at all.

Olivia Flaversham
by Kristina "Curly" Manente

Let's be honest. None of you are surprised it's me writing this one. I don't hide my adoration of *The Great Mouse Detective* from anyone, and I definitely won't hold back my love for the little Scottish doe* that could, Olivia Flaversham.

For those who don't know (and shame on you!) about *The Great Mouse Detective*, let me enlighten you. Also known as *Basil of Baker Street*, *The Great Mouse Detective* is Disney's 26th animated film and tells the adventure of Sherlock-Holmes-admiring Basil and his new found friend and partner, Dr. David Q. Dawson. How do they meet? Well there's no Stamford here, oh no, there's Olivia Flaversham. The movie is their adventure in trying to stop the evil Professor Rattigan, voiced by a brilliant Vincent Price, and save all of Mousedom. It's fabulous and wonderful and full of lots of fun canonical nuggets like Toby and the fact Basil lives under 221B at 221 1/2. It also covers everything from *A Study in Scarlet* to *The Sign of Four* to "The Final Problem." It's a delicious gem of Sherlockiana and I will be perfectly happy if you cease to read this and go watch the movie instead. I'll wait.

Okay, so Olivia Flaversham.

See, her father is a toy maker. I'd say a magic toy maker because damn, he got a toy to dance like a freaking ballerina in the 1800s. Apparently this is one hell of a dangerous profession in the mouse world because he ends up being rather violently kidnapped by a mutilated bat named Fidget, thus scaring hundreds of children to this day. Not to mention it was Olivia's BIRTHDAY! That's just rude.

Yeah, so Daddy is gone and that leaves our little heroine not only alone (because mothers cannot exist in Disney features), but with nothing more to her than her adorable little tartan skirt and a few paintbrushes. So what does she do? Does she mope about and cry and get eaten by the cat of sadness? No! She reads a newspaper and finds out there's a famous detective, and she tracks him down!

Well, she tries. She is just a kid. She gets lost on the way and ends up crying in a boot in the rain. But lucky for her, that's when the kind-hearted Dr. Dawson shows up and brings her to Baker Street, where surely all her problems will be solved.

Except Basil of Baker Street is a straight up douche-nozzle of a mouse that simply doesn't have time for lost fathers. Olivia isn't a pushover though, and she refuses to give up on her dad. Fact is, Basil, Olivia isn't taking any of your crap.

And this is what I love about Olivia. She doesn't care that Basil is this famous detective who loves the sound of his own voice. What she cares about is getting her father back, and she does what it takes and remains brave throughout the entire ordeal … and damn is it an ordeal. She's kidnapped, imprisoned, held as ransom, and has to watch friends and family in danger while her own life is threatened multiple times.

She's a great character. She's a heroine who is young and sometimes foolish, but she's one who remains strong and brave. She is an example of what a heroine should be for young girls. While she's independent, she's not afraid to rely on others for help or show affection, a quality that a lot of modern heroines seem to lack, being presented as *too independent* and refusing any help. She does everything for love, but it's love for her father, not some hot young buck* she only just met (though cheers to Frozen for making fun of this). And while she may feel helpless and scared, she never stops trying. She's also just super sassy.

While the movie may be called *The Great Mouse Detective*, the story is about Olivia. It's her case. She's the one who seems to soften Basil's heart and makes him realize he could do with a friend. Luckily Dawson is there to accept the offer.

Olivia Flaversham is sweet and daring, and also a badass little mouse. So go watch the movie. If you already have, go watch it again, and then read the books by Eve Titus. They don't have Olivia, but I'd be remiss if I didn't recommend them. In short, be as brave as Olivia and maybe rock the big red bow as well. I daresay it's hipster enough.

*A female mouse is called a doe. A male mouse is called a buck. I know, it's weird.

Annie Harrison
by Claire Stemp

In "The Naval Treaty," the first introduction we have to Annie Harrison is through her handwriting. Holmes observes that the letter Watson received from Percy Phelps is in a woman's handwriting – "and a woman of rare character." Holmes goes on to say that "[i]t is something to know that your client is in close contact with someone who for good or evil has an exceptional nature." Given the events of the story, I think Holmes's initial analysis of Annie Harrison's character rings true. She not only remains faithful to her disgraced fiancé, and takes on the role of nurse and protector, but she proves to be of invaluable assistance during the case.

What do we know about Annie Harrison? Her brother, Joseph Harrison, describes her as having nursed Percy Phelps "hand-and-foot this two months back." Considering what we later learn of Joseph's malicious behavior, we might question the validity of his statement, only Percy says words of similar effect: "If it had not been for Miss Harrison here and for the doctor's care, I should not be speaking to you now. She has nursed me by day, and a hired nurse has looked after me by night..." Watson, as is so often the case, focuses on the physical:

"She was a striking-looking woman, a little short and thick for symmetry, but with a beautiful olive complexion, large, dark Italian eyes, and a wealth of deep black hair. Her rich tints made the white face of her companion the more worn and haggard by the contrast." Is Watson's assessment of the un-Englishness of Annie's physical appearance an unconscious slight on her character? In an era of such intense xenophobia, his words might be seen as betraying a degree of unease and distrustfulness. Besides being unsymmetrical, Annie has an olive complexion and "large, dark Italian eyes." Does Annie's nature make her seem foreign in comparison to other English women? Perhaps Watson believes that Annie is beneath his old school chum because, unlike Percy Phelps, she doesn't have connections to powerful men, such as Lord Holdhurst. Should we assume that she is a gold digger who only stuck around to get her hands on her fiancé's money?

We're not supplied with a lot of information about the Harrison siblings' background and circumstances, but there is one detail that is particularly telling. Annie and Joseph's father is an ironmaster. An ironmaster was a manager or, quite often, the owner of a forge or blast furnace that processed iron. He was also an important and affluent man. Annie Harrison and Percy Phelps probably moved in the same circles if they had the opportunity to meet and spend time together. The Phelps family doesn't appear to have any objections to the match. In fact, Percy's parents allow Annie and Joseph to extend their stay during their son's illness and convalescence. I doubt they would have issued such an invitation if they disapproved of the marriage. Of course, as it turns out, neither Lord Holdhurst nor the Phelps family possess any great wealth. Holmes informs Watson that Lord Holdhurst struggles to maintain his position: "He is far from rich, and has many calls. You noticed, of course, that his boots had been re-soled?" After Joseph's burglary attempt, Holmes asks Percy if there is anything in the house that might attract burglars, and Percy says, "[n]othing of value."

Annie's love and devotion for Percy is obvious. Rather than abandoning him to his shame and subsequent illness, Annie stays and nurses Percy back to health. Annie's courage and loyalty doesn't end there. She's determined to see justice done and won't let anyone stand in her way, not even Sherlock Holmes. When Holmes goes off on a philosophical monologue about flowers, it is Annie who confronts him and demands that he return to the matter at hand. In a wonderful exchange between them, Annie asks, "[d]o you see any prospect of

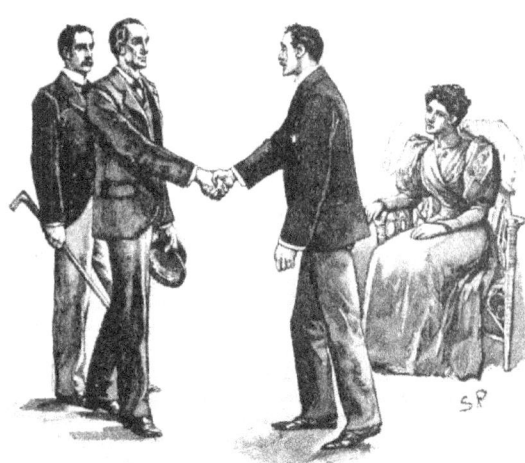

solving this mystery, Mr. Holmes?" When she isn't satisfied with his answer, she says, "Then go to London and test your conclusions." I can't help wondering if Holmes might have been testing Annie to ascertain whether she was truly as honorable as she seemed. At this point, he may have even been debating whether Annie could be an asset to the case.

When Holmes does decide to enlist Annie's assistance, it is a split-second decision. He doesn't have time to explain why he is asking her to spend the day in Percy's sickroom. He can only quickly gain her assent and trust that she will follow his instructions. Annie immediately seems to grasp that her actions will aid the investigation and even plays along with the deception by pretending that she has a headache and would rather stay in the room where it's cooler. Without Annie's help, Holmes wouldn't have been able to lay that trap for Joseph and catch him in the act of breaking into Percy's room to retrieve the naval treaty. Holmes readily acknowledges the debt they owe to Annie: "She carried out every one of my injunctions to the letter, and certainly without her cooperation you would not have that paper in your coat pocket."

While Annie Harrison isn't an adventuress like Irene Adler or a governess thrust into danger like Violet Hunter, she is a strong woman of great integrity. She doesn't flinch from Percy's professional crisis or illness, but faces both head on. While she would never have possessed a career of her own, I would imagine that she provided her full support to Percy throughout his rise in politics. She may have even helped him to advance his career if Percy sought her advice or she played hostess at important social events. Whatever role Annie might have played in the future, I'm sure she played it to perfection.

Eurus Holmes
by Amy Thomas

"There's an east wind coming."

Eurus Holmes is as polarizing a character as the BBC's *Sherlock* has ever produced. Alongside Moriarty, she's the unseen architect of many events throughout Sherlock's life and the series. Many fans suspected a third Holmes sibling throughout the first three seasons of *Sherlock*, but few suspected anything like the person Eurus turned out to be.

She's "the other one," the East Wind, and she provides one of the clearest windows into Sherlock's heart and motivations that the series has ever presented. Not always beloved, but always interesting, she's worth exploring.

Meeting Eurus

Eurus Holmes is foreshadowed throughout *Sherlock* by the impressionistic intrusions of Redbeard and in Mycroft's veiled references to another Holmes sibling, but she bursts fully onto the scene in season four's "The Six Thatchers," when she flirts with John on public transportation. Subsequently, she takes on the role of his therapist and of Sherlock's client, a three-disguise hat trick reminiscent of femme fatales in film noir.

In "The Finale Problem," Eurus reveals her true self, the institutionalized younger sister of Sherlock and Mycroft, whose apparent insanity led her to commit such unspeakable acts as a child, including the murder of Sherlock's childhood friend Victor Trevor, so that she was permanently sent away from the family.

Through games reminiscent of the Saw franchise, and with a mesmeric persona that echoes Sir Anthony Hopkins's Hannibal Lecter in *The Silence of the Lambs*, Eurus unfolds as a larger-than-life antagonist. She knows how to push her brothers to the breaking point, and she uses her knowledge, combined with posthumous help from Moriarty, to break them down piece by piece.

At the same time, the show gives a window into Eurus's own

psyche, though viewers don't know what they're seeing at first. Part of the episode takes place in an airplane that appears to be plummeting toward destruction, with a single child on board to halt the disaster. In the episode's final moments, that child is shown to be Eurus herself, with the plane her own torturous psychological prison.

In season four's last shots of Eurus, she's once again contained, but she's not alone. Sherlock, who throughout the run of the series has overcome his own feelings of alienation, passes on the grace extended to him by John (and to a lesser extent by others) and reaches out to his troubled sister with music, a gift they both share.

Meaning of the Role

Losing the through-line of what Eurus means to the story of *Sherlock* is unfortunately easy because of the many tropes that surround her and visual and textual references to other things that she embodies. Nevertheless, she functions in a very specific way in the story, one that bears investigating: She's a parallel to Sherlock himself.

One of the more jarring aspects of the show for many fans has been the casual use of mental health terms like "psychopath." Much like Doyle's canonical Holmes is said to be cold but isn't, *Sherlock's* titular character is shown, over and over, to be far from the "high-functioning sociopath" he claims to be. Finally, when Eurus appears, the origin of his strangely myopic self-view is revealed. At the beginning of the series, Sherlock believes he is incapable of human connection and friendship; it is Eurus, however, for whom this is actually true. She psychologically poisons those she interacts with, the way Sherlock, before his friendship with John, seemed to believe he did, as if his little sister's issues had seeped into his subconscious at a young age and irrevocably altered his self-view.

The friendship of John through four series teaches Sherlock, not to be human – he was already fully that – but to embrace his entire self, to realize that he's capable of connection with other people on a level he obviously thought was impossible for him. In the end, he chooses to extend that same hope to Eurus, having come full circle to believing that no one is beyond hope.

The writers leave Eurus herself as an enigma. Viewers may never know if Sherlock's embrace of his younger sister and subsequent visits to her actually get through to her troubled mind. The point is that Sherlock has come to believe that it's worth it to try. His question in *The Great Game*: "Will caring about them help save them?" gets a resounding affirmative answer. The man who once thought caring was a disadvantage finally knows that it was Watson's care that saved him, and now caring about Eurus is what enables him to attempt to save her.

In the end, it is Sherlock's character development that matters to the series, far more than Eurus's. Therein lies a potential problem. In a show where extremely intelligent women are most often portrayed as antagonists or criminal masterminds, Eurus is another clever, disturbed woman joining the ranks for the purpose of providing insight into Sherlock. In a show called *Sherlock*, it's reasonable that most other characters are secondary to him in terms of story and screen time, but when multiple female characters exist solely to explain and bounce off him, questions arise about agency and sexism, as well as the use of characters solely as plot devices.

Nevertheless, the final violin duet between Sherlock and Eurus is captivating, and Sian Brooke's powerful portrayal of Eurus refuses to let her fade into the shadows of any of the show's male characters. She's simply too strong of a presence.

Eurus and the Holmes Canon

Finally, Eurus has a stronger connection to the Doyle Canon than may be immediately apparent. In Doyle's "His Last Bow," Holmes famously says, "[t]here's an east wind coming, Watson," meaning the First World War. The story was written as British war effort propaganda, and Holmes goes on to say, "a cleaner, better, stronger land will lie in the sunshine when the storm has cleared."

Eurus, who shares her name with the ancient Greek personification of the East Wind, also starts out as a destructive force, literally obliterating 221B and forcing her brothers and Watson into a deadly trap. In the end, however, she serves as a scalpel that cuts away Sherlock's remaining wounds and reveals him as the full-fledged man and detective he was always meant to be.

Like Doyle's east wind of war, the surgery she performs is painful and ugly, as she uses manipulation and terror to strip away at the layers of her siblings. Without realizing it, though, she does what no one else could – she holds up a mirror to Sherlock Holmes and shows him who he really is, with all of his defenses gone, and he finally sees the reflection of a self he can accept, a person who is stronger and better than he ever thought he could be.

In hindsight, it's difficult to feel fully at peace with the idea of the canonical Holmes's espousal of one of history's deadliest wars. Similarly, it's psychologically challenging to accept the idea that Eurus's sadistic antagonism ends up serving a positive purpose. No doubt, readers will continue to debate the concepts of "His Last Bow" for years to come, and in a similar way, viewers of *Sherlock* will continue to debate and wrestle with the compelling, difficult character of Eurus Holmes.

Molly Hooper
by Amy Thomas

Long, straight hair, lipstick that comes and goes, and an ironically macabre career – exploring unassuming but totally awesome Molly Hooper is a journey that starts with specific stories framed by the creators of the BBC's *Sherlock*, finds its anchor in the Sherlock Holmes canon as a whole, and winds up the wider genre of procedural mysteries.

At the beginning of *A Study in Pink*, Molly Hooper is first introduced as a contrast to and amplifier of Sherlock's character. His abrupt, almost alien behavior as he flogs a corpse and fails to notice any normal social signals is contrasted sharply with Molly's slight attempt at humor and shy flirtation. She immediately gives the viewer a window into the detective's differences from the rest of the world – a world where a woman's attempt to impress a man with lipstick would be appreciated at best and ignored at worst. In Sherlock's world, however, facts come first, no matter what, even when it comes to the size of a woman's mouth. At the same time, Molly shows herself to be more persevering than one might expect, since she doesn't give up on Sherlock.

In *The Blind Banker*, Molly again amplifies Sherlock's character, this time helping to show that he is not always quite as socially oblivious as one might expect and not above cashing in on relationships to get what he wants. His blatant flirting with her in the cafeteria line not only works on a general level by capturing her attention and flattering her (a certain amount of investment in the relationship for the future), but it also leads to an immediate look at a body that he needs to see in order to complete his investigation. Though Molly appears to be completely under Sherlock's spell in this instance, readers of her blog, which is produced by the BBC and considered to be part of the Sherlock canon, will have encountered the following quote:

"Oh, and Sherlock came in again tonight. And he was his usual arrogant self! And he was blatantly flirting with me and I know he's doing it and I should tell him to stop but I don't! And, of course, he was only doing it so I'd help him with something. As soon as he got what he wanted, he was off."

Molly may intermittently act as Sherlock's dupe, but she's not an entirely oblivious victim.

Along with other major arcs of the series, Molly's story comes to a head first in *The Great Game*, when she is shown to be the unwitting pawn of two extremely clever men, neither of whom is terribly scrupulous about using her for his own ends. Sherlock once again hurts her by abruptly pointing out that her boyfriend is gay, though his offensiveness is apparently unintentional in this case. Jim's use of her is far colder and more sinister, as she becomes a part of his deadly game.

The cliffhanger at the end of the series leaves Molly hanging as much as the other characters – a woman with a preference for two men who use her, but at the same time a competent career woman who isn't as gullible as she seems.

Through the next two series, her character grows enormously. The revelation of Molly's true importance in Sherlock's second series, particularly throughout *The Reichenbach Fall*, certainly met and then exceeded fans' wildest hopes. Previously, Molly's humiliation at the Christmas party in *A Scandal in Belgravia* had revealed an unexpectedly contrite, even sweet, side of Holmes. Later on, her perceptiveness regarding his true mental state ("You look sad when you think he can't see you") helped him to understand her value. Finally, in the end, when even Watson had to be kept in the dark, Holmes looked to her for help.

By series three, Molly has become a formidable ally for Sherlock and a woman who realizes her own strength to the point that she's willing to take him to task for his substance abuse. Also, through windows into Sherlock's mind palace, she's shown to be a permanent part of his mental processes, his respect of her so great that she represents all medical knowledge to him.

Finally, series four makes Molly an emotional touchstone in a heartbreaking way, when, through Eurus Holmes's manipulation, Sherlock is forced to declare his love for her or risk her death. This final major scene between the two friends divided fans, but again showed Molly's emotional complexity and the coexistence of her vulnerability and fierceness. The season's last shot of Molly is a happy one, but viewers are left to imagine the difficulty of repairing her fractured emotions.

In the first series of Sherlock, Molly was a humorous character with a great deal of potential. In the subsequent series, she revealed her true nature as a multi-faceted, faithful, and intelligent woman. Her future in the show, if it continues, is certainly something to anticipate.

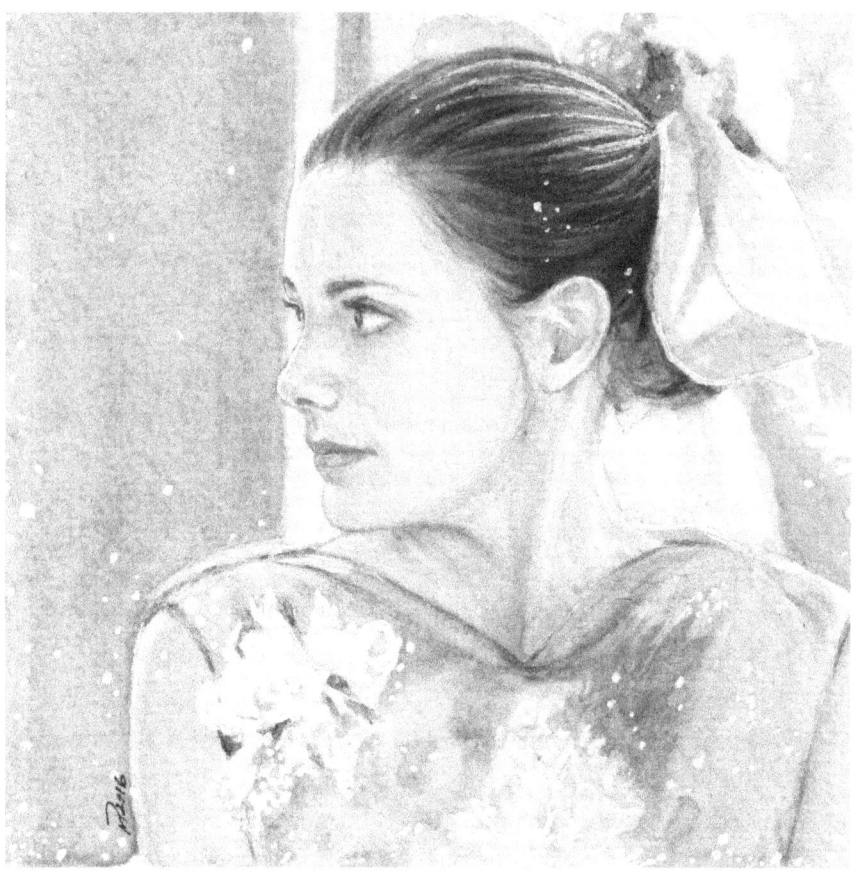

Molly and the Holmes Canon

Virtually every incarnation of Sherlock Holmes shares the common characteristic of willingness to use innocent people to accomplish his own ends, and the BBC version expresses this quality no more ruthlessly than his original predecessor. Most of Sherlock's flaws – such as pipe smoking, drug use, and some aspects of his sociopathy – have been portrayed as glamorous and attractive in various books and films, to the point that in many cases, they have become like backhanded strengths.

His selfish, borderline-exploitation of other people, as exemplified in his treatment of Molly, however, is impossible to glamorize.

In simple terms, at the beginning of the series, Molly showed the viewer an ugly side of Sherlock, one that is absolutely necessary to the character. Without true flaws, Sherlock Holmes is a caricature – an impossibly heroic genius who is good at everything and even successfully controls his vices. Molly's frequent presence on the show is a reminder that the world's only consulting detective can be selfish, thoughtless, and occasionally cruel. He may be a hero, but he is also an anti-hero, a duality that makes him one of the most intriguing characters in the world.

As the series progresses, however, Molly's growth takes her from a dupe to a queen, a woman whose ability to stand up for herself and for what is best for her friends ultimately affects Sherlock's own character. He becomes a better person as a result of trusting and knowing her.

Molly and the Mystery Genre

The concept of flawed heroes runs through all of literature, film, and television, but mystery novels and shows have made the concept of the heroic antihero an art form. Larger-than-life detectives bring larger-than-life vices to the cases they solve. Dr. House has his Vicodin, Flavia de Luce her vindictiveness, Adrian Monk his obsessive compulsions. Arguably, most of these characters are the descendents of Sherlock Holmes, attempts by authors to capture the complex interplay of light and dark that makes up Conan Doyle's hero. The creators of the BBC's *Sherlock* have seen fit to soften their hero's smoking habit and take away his drug use almost entirely. Molly is essential to the show because she highlights what makes Sherlock so very imperfect – his frequent lack of understanding of people or concern for them. The things she amplifies in him make him a reflection not only of Conan Doyle's original source, but also of the mystery genre as a whole, a gray-shaded world of flawed heroes. And yet, there's something a little bit different about Molly Hooper, a little bit independent, a little bit unwilling to give up, something in her that ends up surprising even Sherlock Holmes.

Lady Hilda Trelawney Hope
by Lyndsay Faye

Lady Hilda Trelawney Hope, apparently the "most lovely woman in London" in addition to being one hell of a Secret Agent Super Spy, might not at first blush seem the perfect choice for a Femme Friday. After all, Lady Hilda steals the impolitic diplomatic letter left in her husband's charge with apparently no greater trouble than if she had been rifling through his loose change to run down the corner store and pick up some cigarettes. She is one of two criminals in "The Second Stain," she the thief and Eduardo Lucas the blackmailer who compels her to theft; but I would argue that she is one of the most formidable women in sixty tales, and in my headcanon, every month or so she goes out for three-martini lunches with the unnamed woman who turned Charles Augustus Milverton into Swiss cheese.

We meet her in high Watsonian fashion, with our good doctor waxing still more than usually poetic over Lady Hilda's "subtle, delicate charm" and the "beautiful colouring of that exquisite head," and her "queenly presence," which was "tall, graceful, and intensely womanly." (My new goal in life is for my presence to be "intensely womanly," which I wonder quite how best to accomplish short of wearing my ovaries as epaulettes.) While Watson adjusts his trousers discreetly, Holmes treats his unexpected visitor with remarkable courtesy – no, he says, he cannot reveal the full import of her husband Trelawney Hope's visit, but the missing material could well cause Hope's political career, if not all of Europe, to go tits up.

Lady Hilda is sincere and persuasive; though terrified, she is poised and composed. She cleverly chooses the one chair in the room which will afford her privacy by lighting her from the back, and after Holmes gives his regretful denials, she neither berates him nor even disagrees with his principles. All told, it is a curious interview indeed for a noblewoman in desperate straits to carry on with a Bohemian hired detective, and both parties treat each other with considerable respect.

It is not until Holmes and Watson are invited to the murdered Eduardo Lucas's crime scene by a delightfully warm Lestrade that we learn Lady Hilda is a full metal badass in combat boots. After being told that Trelawney Hope could be ruined, Lady Hilda – whose only thought was for her husband in the first place, as she was convinced the "foolish letter, a letter of an impulsive, loving girl" would be in her husband's eyes "criminal" if revealed – promptly decides to don a disguise, create a secret identity as a typist with a taste for gore, and wheedle her way into the room where the letter was hidden. She next pretends to faint in front of the constable, thereby easily ridding herself of him, steals her own letter back, dusts her hands and mucks up the placement of the carpet, and is off home again before you can say "ninja." One wonders where women of the peerage learn such sweet moves.

What troubles me most about this whole scenario is how obviously Lady Hilda loves her husband and how much she is willing to sacrifice for him when this Trelawney chappie is, let us be real here, kind of a power tool. First off, his name is "Trelawney." Second, it's certainly reasonable for a diplomat dealing with scads of sensitive information to neglect to confide in his wife high matters of state; but the way he completely dismisses her from that aspect of his life is disappointing to anyone who has ever watched *House of Cards*. Finally, Lady Hilda is so certain that he would reject her upon learning of her past that I feel confident in labeling him an asshat. Lady Hilda is being alternately ignored and abused by the men in this story, and despite the direness of her situation, she navigates all with intentions fully rooted in loyalty and love.

When Holmes confronts Lady Hilda about the theft, she rebuffs him completely – not once, but *six times in a goddamn row*. This is

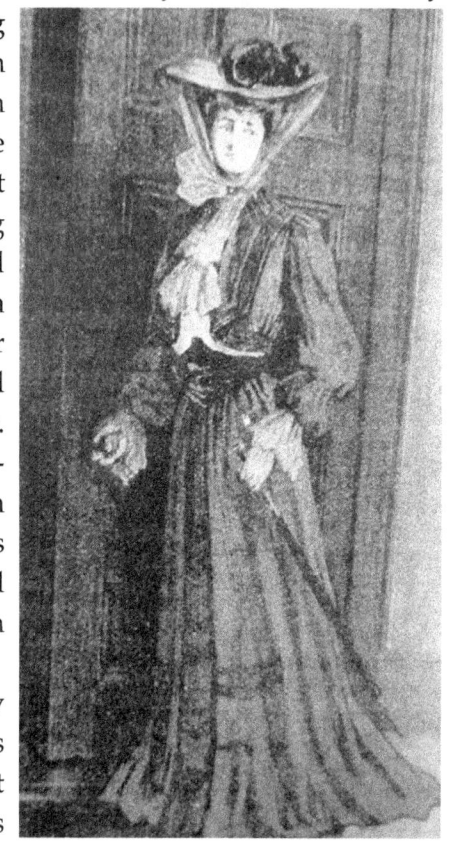

Sherlock Holmes we're talking about here – you know, that fella whose orders are almost impossible to ignore? Fortunately, Lady Hilda at last decides to enlist Holmes's help, seeing as Sherlock Holmes thinks about as highly of blackmailers as he does chigger bites. After Holmes arranges for the letter to magically reappear and this Trelawney sap scampers off like a rabbit to show it to the wife he just ordered out of the room, all is well again, and one supposes that this mental banana peel will never imagine his spouse has a knack for international espionage. As for Sherlock Holmes and Dr. Watson – they sure as hell is toasty know better.

Rachel Howells
by Fabienne Courouge

Rachel Howells has been overlooked in most scholarly works and adaptations. I guess that originally old manors, ancestral riddles and treasure hunts aroused much more interest than the unfathomable meandering of a woman's soul. And, to be fair, Sherlock Holmes himself is the first one to not recognise her role in the mystery.

Not paying much attention, he overlooks her brain fever that "the careful reader will recognise [...] as one, not of the brain, but of a more susceptible organ, the heart" ("The Musgrave Ritual: An Alternate Solution," Jack Harville, *BSJ*, 30:201).

Even the comment on her "excitable Welsh temperament" and her "hysterical attack" are ignored in favour of the highly exciting puzzle of the ritual. But beneath the surface, beneath the historical quest and the connection to Charles I, beneath the cryptic Ritual itself, lies a story of love, obsession, betrayal, and of revenge. The key to the mystery lies in the depth of Rachel's heart, and had Holmes kept a careful eye on her, he wouldn't have had to decipher abstruse ancient mumbo-jumbo and solve trigonometry problems to find the treasure (okay... it would have been a very short short-story then). Holmes was young at that time, and knew little about sentiment (which, concerning the detective, is the hell of an understatement) and she was a maid, one of those women you "see but you don't observe"; the kind of woman you make use of without a second thought. (Let's remember Holmes's flippant engagement to Milverton's maid.)

The early adaptations didn't grant much more consideration to Rachel. She's been used (again) as a narrative device. Although she's convicted of murder and theft in Georges Tréville's 1912 silent movie *Le trésor des Musgrave*, she's not even given a name, but only called "the young maid." In *Sherlock Holmes Faces Death* (1943), loosely based on "The Musgrave Ritual," she's nothing but Brunton's secret wife and accomplice.

44

But Rachel is so much more, and her history deserves more than to be considered as "put there to add length, intrigue, and complication to the real story" Christopher Redmond furthermore regrets "that Doyle, though he gives her a brief and melodramatic mad scene, does not have her attack Miss Tregellis as well as Brunton. But then it is equally disappointing that Doyle did not treat this incident of murder motivated by jealousy in a story of its own, rather than touching on it in confusion with the story of the noble family and its royal secret" (Christopher Redmond, *In Bed with Sherlock Holmes*, p. 108).

She's a wild and passionate character as Conan Doyle liked to present foreign women in his stories (just as Anna Coram, Maria Gibson, Mme Henri Fournaye; see Nancy Talburt's article named "Sherlock Holmes and the Liberated Woman" in: *Canon Fodder*, pp. 82-97) and Rachel is Welsh (which can be translated as meaning "not as civilized as English people"). She's dark, silent and brooding just as she is bold and careless when she escapes her room to get to the pond. She's made of the stuff of criminal female lovers that the world views with a mix of horror and fascination.

And Conan Doyle, through Holmes's voice, wonders "[w]hat smouldering fire of vengeance had suddenly sprung into flame in this passionate Celtic woman's soul when she saw the man who had wronged her – wronged her, perhaps, far more than we suspected – in her power." Rachel is, ultimately, one of the few incandescent and merciless women of the canon (we could also classify Kitty Winter, Maria Gibson and Isadora Klein under such heading). The women who stand out so starkly in the polished Victorian era. She's a tragic heroine. Jeremy Paul, who dramatized the adventure for the Granada *Sherlock Holmes* adaptation, saw it clearly, making Rachel the central figure, opening and closing the episode with close-up on Johanna Kirby, who plays Rachel's part.

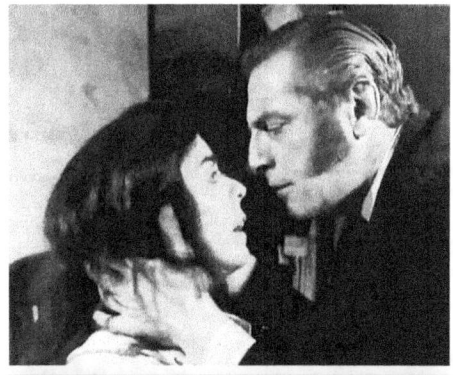

She's Bonnie Parker, challenging the establishment and committing crimes for love. "With my brains and your heart what do we want with service to others when a world is out there calling us, my love?"

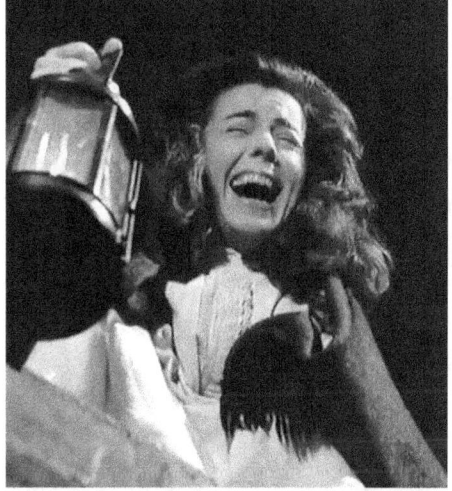

She's revengeful Medea, spiralling into madness and committing murder when she feels betrayed.

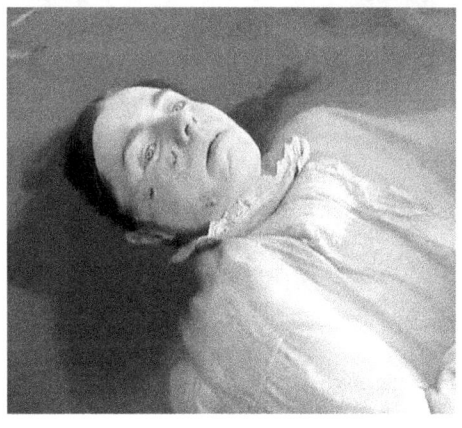

And although Holmes presumes that "[v]ery probably she's far away from Hurlstone now and carries her secret with her," she's shown as Ophelia, dead of love and grief, floating in the brook.

(Granada Television. *The Musgrave Ritual*, 41'10"; 44'12"; 50'27")

Mrs. Hudson
by Maria Fleischhack

"Mrs. Hudson leave Baker Street? England would fall!"

This quote from Sherlock's *A Scandal Belgravia* sums up one of the most important characters in the Sherlock Holmes stories and adaptations. Mrs. Hudson is by the far the most patient, resilient, organized and brave women in the canon, and while we often wonder how John Watson manages to stay with Sherlock Holmes (without killing him or at least plotting his murder a couple of times), I found myself asking that question even more often where Mrs. Hudson is concerned. In "The Dying Detective," Watson describes her as a long-suffering woman who adored Sherlock Holmes and never once interfered with his work out of respect, no matter how insane it seemed. Irene Adler might be the Woman to Sherlock Holmes, but Mrs. Hudson is the Superwoman.

Interestingly, we don't know a lot about her from the stories. We know that her first name could possibly be Martha, but probably isn't, we know that she might or might not be Scottish, and we know that she has the patience of an angel, because she stays with Holmes and Watson through thick and thin – or should I say, through gunshots and temper tantrums.

Sherlock Holmes and John Watson need her in many different ways. In the books she starts off as the landlady, but soon is firmly established as the housekeeper as well, who keeps a staff of maids and a page, Billy. You will have noticed that despite her protests, she is very much landlady *and* housekeeper of Sherlock and John in the BBC series. In fact, in the stories and many adaptations she's not only the landlady/housekeeper, but also a cook, nurse, 'mother', psychic, magician, super sleuth and Sherlock's most prominent critic. When she appears in the stories, she is usually introducing a new guest or client and very often she shows how little she appreciates the visitors Holmes receives (she's especially suspicious of the Baker Street Irregulars). Nevertheless, she serves the clients tea, water, gin or jewels, depending on the occasion.

I especially love Rosalie Williams's portrayal of Mrs. Hudson in the

Granada Holmes series, because she talks back, which is a glorious thing to witness. While she might let Sherlock Holmes do whatever he bloody well wants – such as shooting the wall, filling his flat with poisonous fumes and playing loud music in the middle of the night – she makes sure that Holmes knows how she feels about it. Granada's Mrs. Hudson is very much about non-verbal communication and her sass is something which even Martin Freeman's John Watson could learn from. Geraldine James's Mrs. Hudson in Guy Ritchie's *Sherlock Holmes* films is also appropriately done with Holmes's antics.

Una Stubbs's Mrs. Hudson takes the cake of course. We've never had an alcoholic, marijuana-smoking, exotic-dancing, Aston-Martin-driving, and phone-in-bra-hiding Mrs. Hudson before and I have yet to meet a single person who doesn't love her (possibly Mycroft, but even he kinda adores her, I bet). We love her, because despite all the trouble Sherlock

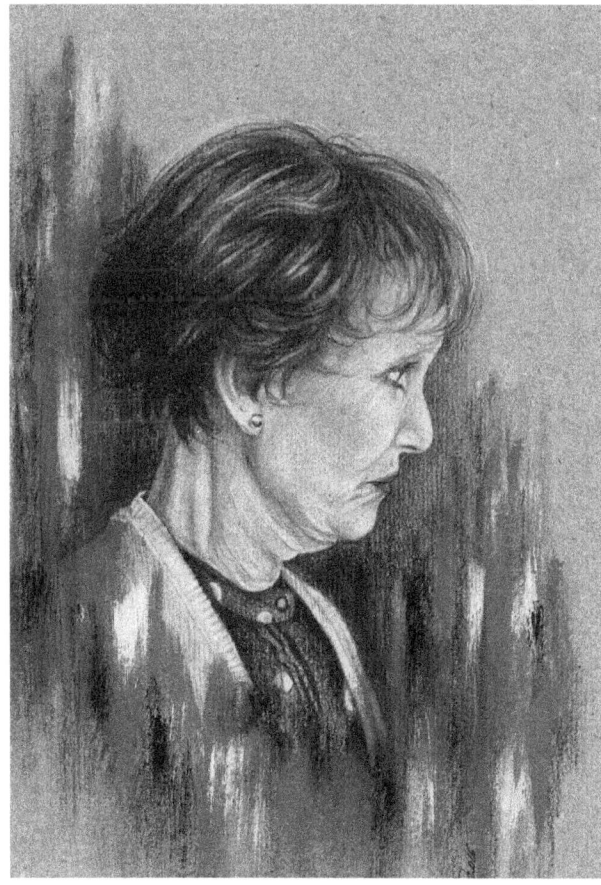

causes, and despite his often offensive behavior (think of the little episode in the beginning of *Hounds of Baskerville*), she loves her boys and very much acts like a mother hen. To me, one of the loveliest scenes in the BBC series with Mrs. Hudson is when Mycroft tells her to shut up and John and Sherlock are simply scandalized. Sherlock will defend her to his death (though he will claim the privilege of shouting at his landlady every now and then).

Another kick ass Mrs. Hudson features in *Elementary* as Ms Hudson played by Candis Cayne. An expert in ancient Greek, Ms Hudson is a transgender woman who used to be a Boy Scout. In return for being able to stay with Sherlock and Joan during a snow storm after a breakup, she organizes Sherlock's book shelves and helps to build a fire in the fireplace. She has, however, only featured in three episodes so far and her confidence and skills would definitely be welcome in further episodes.

One particular episode in the canon shows Mrs. Hudson's dedication to her demanding lodger: In "The Empty House," Mrs. Hudson goes as far as to put her own life in danger for Sherlock Holmes. She crawls around on her knees to move around the wax figure which Holmes has placed in his living room in order to make Colonel Moran believe that it is the detective who sits in his chair while being fully aware that Moran will shoot at Holmes's wax double. In a similar way, Mrs. Hudson ends up in danger when the CIA agents break into 221B Baker Street in search of Irene Adler's phone in *A Scandal in Belgravia* and what does she do? Hudders ain't afraid of no CIA. Watch her hide that phone in her bra, because that's how she rolls. Ladies and gents, Mrs. Hudson: Badass of Baker Street.

Violet Hunter
by Sarah Roy

Violet Hunter is the client in "The Copper Beeches", the final story in *The Adventures of Sherlock Holmes*. In addition to introducing us to this lady who knows she is pretty darn rockin' and isn't afraid to casually mention it, the story also provides a good dose of perspective for all of us who have ever feared that this new haircut may have been a horrible, life-altering mistake.

Our story begins with Holmes in a strop. He knows his world has hit rock bottom, and that the criminals of the world will never provide him with entertainment again. His evidence: a letter from a young woman asking to consult on whether or not she should take a position as a governess. Enter Miss Violet Hunter, her courage, her self-confidence, and her amazing hair.

Despite the impression Holmes took from her letter, Violet is not an indecisive person who has to poll the audience before doing anything. The job she has been offered comes with a great salary (more than double her last position) and what appears to be not a lot of work. The one problem is the extremely weird person who wants to hire her. As soon as she walks into the employment agency, Jephro Rucastle checks her out and declares her "accomplishments" perfect for the job. She counters that her, um, accomplishments may be less than he imagines and rattles off things that were considered proper accomplishments for a lady of the time: a little French and German, music, etc. And by the way my eyes – and brain! – are up here, buddy. Since you're pretending to want to hire me for said brain.

The job is caring for only one child. Oh, and his wife is "faddy" and may want her to wear a certain blue dress and sit a certain way and little things like that. But that's no big deal, right? Oh, and your fabulous chestnut hair is just the sort of thing we're into but cut it really short because we like it that way. We the readers, having watched many crime shows and generally been told to trust our instincts when it comes to creepy old men, think we know where this is going. We would probably feel safer taking our chances against unemployment and starvation than follow this guy to his middle-of-nowhere house.

Miss Hunter, however, has never watched *CSI* and doesn't care. She declines the offer not only because she has every right to be creeped out but because Rucastle and his "faddy" wife do not properly appreciate the gloriousness that is her hair and want it gone before they will employ her. A girl has to set limits somewhere. However, after a couple days of thinking and a couple more bills turning up in the post, she has to face the reality that her hair is not going to do her any real good if she is literally living on the street. But she does want a second opinion from someone who knows a thing or two. With no family or friends, she has turned to Holmes for his widely-known ability to make sense out of weird stuff. Holmes, after listening to her story, apparently can make

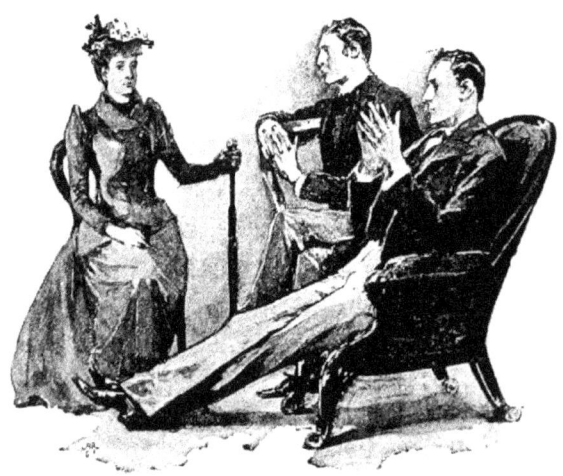

very little sense of it. He sends her off telling her not to worry but if she is in danger to fire off a telegram and he will come charging in to aid her. She isn't too happy with this "danger" business but goes anyway because she doesn't have a lot of options. However, our girl Violet is not one to sit around and let a mystery go unsolved, especially when all the weird stuff is happening to her personally. Using her own observational powers (which she is not afraid to brag about later, because let's face it, she does pretty well), she manages to gather quite a lot of evidence of even more strange goings-on – a man lurking in the bushes, shuttered tower rooms, and hair that looks exactly like hers hidden in a drawer. However, she does not call on Holmes until she is justly terrified by strange shadows moving in the attic and her employer is threatening her with a giant dog.

Holmes and Watson arrive and as usual Holmes deduces the evidence into a coherent story, but it is up to Violet to actually get things done. She has come this far on her own and so Holmes assigns her the role of disposing of anyone who might get in the way of solving the mystery. Now that she has braved the creepy house and creepier people, gathered the evidence, brought Holmes there when the Rucastles are conveniently going out, and temporarily removed everyone else who would get in their way, it is up to Holmes and Watson to do the serious investigative work of kicking down doors, holding a gun, and jumping to an incorrect conclusion about where the formerly imprisoned Alice Rucastle has gone.

Holmes calls Violet Hunter a "quite exceptional woman" and Watson, bless his romantic heart, is convinced that this is the woman for Holmes. Watson, however, is doomed to be disappointed. Holmes is not interested despite being duly impressed with her cleverness and courage. However, this is just as well since Violet Hunter remains perfectly capable of making her own way in the world, soon becoming head of a private school and meeting with "considerable success." If courage is not the absence of fear but being afraid and charging ahead anyway, then Violet Hunter is indeed as courageous as she is pragmatic, observant, and resourceful.

The Irregular Girls
by Amy Thomas

This essay is a little bit different. It's not about one character; it's about the girls that are not given names in the Doyle stories, yet they're some of the most important people in the entire Holmesian world. Who do I mean? The resourceful, clever young women who round out the ranks of the Baker Street Irregulars, Sherlock Holmes's network of tiny spies throughout the city of London. Adults are conspicuous. In Victorian London, where street children were a dime a dozen, Holmes's irregulars went places adults couldn't go and saw and heard things adults never could have discovered.

The Irregulars feature early on in the Holmes canon, with brief but colorful appearances in *A Study in Scarlet* and *The Sign of Four*. From these accounts, we learn that Sherlock Holmes is in the habit of employing street children, under the command of a snarky chap named Wiggins, to be his eyes and ears in the city, and that he pays them well. In a more personal way, Holmes's patiently tolerant interactions with the children provide a brief but very warm window into his heart.

Of the Irregulars themselves, little detail is provided, but as with so many things in Doyle's writing, what isn't said proves as intriguing as what is actually written. The brief accounts of the Irregulars have spawned entire juvenile book series and the main plot of a recent made-for-TV- film starring Jonathan Pryce, as well as countless mentions in Holmes pastiche novels and films.

One reason for this seems to be the age at which many of us first meet Sherlock Holmes. Even in their youngest days, Holmes and Watson seemed old to me when I read about them at the ripe age of ten. The Irregulars, however, weren't so far removed. They were kids, like me, and through their eyes, I could better understand Holmes and the Victorian world.

Modern adaptations like *Sherlock* tend to go a different route. In Doyle's day, giving street children wage-paying labor was a kindness. Today, it wouldn't play the same way, so Holmes is given a homeless network instead. However, *The Sign of Three* did pay homage to the detective's way with children through his amusing and heartwarming interactions with Archie.

To truly appreciate the female members of the Baker Street Irregulars requires a liberal measure of imagination. We meet them in the genteel environs of 221B, but that is neither their home nor their usual environment. Through no fault of their own, these girls are on the street, but they're far from helpless. Instead of giving up, they choose to take a job that is exciting and dangerous in equal measure, from a no less eccentric man. They are trusted to be sharp-eyed, stealthy, and resourceful, and they are – true unsung heroines of the Holmes stories.

Much has been said before about issues of sexism and feminism in the Doyle stories. Often cited for consideration is Holmes's declaration that Mary Morstan (later Watson) has potential as a detective. What very few people ever seem to point out is how absolutely equalized the accounts of the Irregulars are. Not only did Holmes say a woman had *potential* to be a detective, but he was arguably already employing women as *detectives*, albeit very young ones.

If they were a little bit less intriguing, the Baker Street Irregulars might be relegated to Sherlockian footnote status, but they're just too interesting for that. It's impossible to imagine a time when they will fail to make their mark in books and on film, right alongside Holmes himself.

Isadora Klein
by Alexandra Christian

Everyone knows Irene Adler. If you ask any Sherlockian worth their salt: "what about the women in the Holmes canon?" the first thing out of their well-read mouths will be Irene Adler. It seems that everyone remembers "The Woman." The one woman that could possibly have held Sherlock Holmes's heart or at least his intellectual interest. A perfect foil. But one can't forget that there are hosts of other women in the canon that prove to be worthy characters.

Case in point: Isadora Klein. It isn't surprising that more people don't remember her. She's featured in a lesser known story, "The Adventure of the Three Gables" (1926), that appeared in *The Casebook of Sherlock Holmes*. By this time, the world in which Sherlock Holmes had lived was all but gone and Conan Doyle was trying to keep up. To that end, in Isadora Klein he created a female antagonist that would be very much at home in a speakeasy. I contend that Klein was a Noir *femme fatale* well before the genre had been popularized by such authors as Dashiell Hammett and Elmore Leonard.

In "The Adventure of the Three Gables," Holmes and Watson are engaged by a Mary Maberley to investigate several strange incidents at her home The Three Gables. During her meeting with Holmes, Mrs. Maberley reveals that her son, Douglas, passed away in Rome after ending a tragic love affair. Shortly after, a man arrived at Maberley's home offering a handsome price to buy her home and everything in it. Maberley and her lawyer, Sutro, find it very strange that, should she accept the offer, nothing could be removed from the home. When she protested, the man canceled the deal, and Maberley contacted Holmes. In true Holmes fashion, he sets Mrs. Maberley and Mr. Sutro up as bait, figuring that whatever it is the man desired, he would get it through criminal means since the deal to buy it fell through. The house is burgled in the night, but Mrs. Maberley manages to grab a piece of the only thing stolen – a manuscript for a tawdry romance novel that her son had planned to publish starring his ex-lover, Isadora Klein.

Isadora is described as once being a "celebrated beauty" that no woman could touch. Even now, approaching middle-age (Oh the horror!), she's still commanding much-younger lovers and breaking hearts as "the richest as well as the most lovely widow on Earth." And all talk of beauty aside, Isadora is crafty and devious, perhaps more so than even the infamous Irene Adler. She doesn't appear until the climax of the story, like so many Holmes villains, but reading her spar with Holmes is perhaps the model of banter to which all writers should aspire.

Holmes, ever the arrogant ass, assumes that his scrawled note, *"Shall it be the police, then?"* will shock the lady into confessing all, but for all his cleverness he fails to deduce that a woman who would gladly flaunt her sexual exploits all over Europe will probably not be shocked by an idle threat. She pretends, of course, but when Holmes accuses her of hiring the burglars, she doesn't immediately throw herself at his feet to beg for mercy. In fact, she turns to her most effective skill: she tries to seduce him with false flattery and her "charming coquettish" smiles. She's also smart enough to play on Holmes's sensibilities, expecting that he won't reveal her role in the strange happenings at Mrs. Maberley's home as he is a gentleman that would never disgrace a lady. And she's right. Rather than go to the police, Holmes essentially blackmails Isadora into paying off Mrs. Maberley in exchange for his silence. This is quite telling, as we know from poor Charles Augustus Milverton, that Holmes saves his most savage loathing for blackmailers. Blackmailing Isadora is likely the worst insult that Holmes could think of. Gentleman indeed!

Isadora's greatest crime in the end, it seems, is her rejection of Douglas Maberley. He wasn't interested in being Isadora's boy toy that she could take or leave. He wanted to be her one and only lover, and when she cast him aside, his madness drove him to pen the scandalous novel that she was so desperate to steal. It painted Isadora as a heartless vixen that had used Maberley like an old handkerchief. That would very much hinder her socialite dating schedule, so she used her feminine wiles to engage a group of ruffians to not only threaten Sherlock Holmes to stay out of it, but also to acquire the manuscript at all costs: those same "good hounds" that she had hired months before to beat Douglas Maberley in order to drive him away from her. To Conan Doyle and his targeted readers, Isadora Klein was an ultimate villain – a woman who rejects the idea of motherhood and feminine morality. A woman who does what she likes, with whomever she likes.

In the end, Holmes doesn't turn Klein over to the police, but insists that she pay off Mrs. Maberley for her trouble, seeming to scold her for her devious ways. That indicates to me that Isadora is likely a result of Conan Doyle's own view of the changing world: the proper Victorian lady giving way to the 1920s flapper with her short skirts and loose morality. In short, Isadora Klein was the embodiment of everything a man of the early twentieth century feared: intelligent, independent, and capable of beating them at their own games.

Martha
by Maria Fleischhack

Why is so little known about female spies and why do they so seldom appear in spy novels of the first decades of the twentieth century, never mind in reports on spies (at least not until recently, when proper research was conducted)? The answer is simple: Women were not seriously considered to be good spies – lacking patriotism and being too emotional and obviously falling in love with the men they were supposed to spy on – or so the common story goes. Fact is, a lot of women worked as spies in WWI and after, but they did what many men did not. They kept their mouths shut and simply went back to their normal lives after the work was done, not seeking medals or recognition. Not being taken seriously always proves to be of advantage, as Holmes's Baker Street Irregulars will tell you.

One of these forgotten figures plays a crucial role in Sherlock Holmes's final case, "His Last Bow": Martha, Von Bork's housekeeper (whose name may or may have been based on Belgian spy Marthe Cnockaert McKenna, though there is zero proof for this and it's merely a guess that Doyle might have heard of the court case against her in 1916). Occasionally she is thought to be a very loyal Mrs. Hudson who stayed in the employ of Holmes long after he left Baker Street. More likely she was a very promising spy in the making, whom Holmes met in preparation for his case against the German spy Von Bork. Martha lives in the household of the spy, who seems to be one of the best and therefore most dangerous ones in Britain (because he needs to be a good adversary for Holmes to finally beat – this story was, after all, supposed to kindle the hope for a British triumph in the middle of WWI). She is a silent and reliable servant. She knows Von Bork's family and the man intimately, and keeps track of his visitors and correspondences of all kinds. Yet, she is taken to be simply a good housekeeper, never giving cause for suspicion and remaining behind even when Von Bork evacuates his family to Germany upon the impending war.

Baron Von Herling and Von Bork avidly discuss what it means to be a good spy (which includes being able to hold your liquor, being a playboy and being good at all kinds of sports) – and yet they completely underestimate the capabilities of the only servant left in Von Bork's employ.

> Only one window showed a light behind them; in it there stood a lamp, and beside it, seated at a table, was a dear old ruddy-faced woman in a country cap. She was bending over her knitting and stopping occasionally to stroke a large black cat upon a stool beside her. [...] 'She might almost personify Britannia,' said he, 'with her complete self-absorption and general air of comfortable somnolence.'

It appears that 'typical female behavior' is all it takes to fool one of the best. Once Holmes, as Altamont, the Irish-American spy for the Germans, manages to subdue Von Bork, he has Watson ring the bell for her.

> 'There is no one in the house except old Martha, who has played her part to admiration. I got her the situation here when first I took the matter up. Ah, Martha, you will be glad to hear that all is well.'
> The pleasant old lady had appeared in the doorway. She curtseyed with a smile to Mr. Holmes, but glanced with some apprehension at the figure upon the sofa. 'It is all right, Martha. He has not been hurt at all.'
> 'I am glad of that, Mr. Holmes. According to his lights he has been a kind master. He wanted me to go with his wife to Germany yesterday, but that would hardly have suited your plans, would it, sir?'

Can you hear the snark? That lady is full of snark, and she knows she's been indispensable to Holmes.

> 'No, indeed, Martha. So long as you were here I was easy in my mind. We waited some time for your signal to-night. [...] I saw your lamp go out and knew that the coast was clear. You can report to me to-morrow in London, Martha, at Claridge's Hotel.'
> 'Very good, sir.'

'I suppose you have everything ready to leave.'

'Yes, sir. He posted seven letters to-day. I have the addresses as usual.'

That is that. Without making a fuss of any sort, Martha leaves the scene, gets her things (and probably the cat), and most likely receives her debriefing from Holmes the next morning before moveing on to whatever is next in her life. She never looks back.

I like to imagine her becoming one of the matrons who taught and aided all of those ladies on the home front, and who lived long enough to see women get the right to vote.

It is evident that Altamont, aka Sherlock Holmes, manages to trick Von Bork not only into sending false military plans to Germany, but to capture him while showing off his *Practical Handbook of Bee Culture* to Watson in the most over-the-top way imaginable, followed by one of the most memorable conversations with his friend at the end of the story. However, it is Martha, inconspicuous and yet of inestimable value to Holmes and the British government, who leaves without a trace, her success to be reaped by others, like so many of her occupation and gender. In a way, she mirrors the young Holmes of *A Study in Scarlet*, who works for the sake of *the work* and whose attitude eventually convinces Watson to write down his adventures so that he will be recognized for his work. But Martha knows her own value, and Holmes trusts her implicitly, and that makes Martha quite a special woman.

Mary Morstan
by Lyndsay Faye

Let's chat about Mary Morstan for a sec. No, not that one, the one you're thinking of we'll get to in a wee bit. I'm talking first about the one who kicked so much canonical ass that she deserved her own spinoff series. (Does this exist? Tell me, please, if it happens to exist.)

One of the most canny tricks they teach actors is also a neat tip for writing fiction of all types: listening to what other characters have to say about your character can be a much better guideline and way more insightful than the things your character says about him- or herself. Take Sherlock Holmes, for example. Sherlock Holmes talks mad phat game about prizing reason above all things. "I should never marry myself, lest I bias my judgment"; "I am a brain, Watson. The rest of me is a mere appendix"; *I haz no feels and you can't make me haz teh feels.*

But then Watson has to go and write down all those moments when Holmes was snortchuckling over hiding a treaty in a curry dish, or scritching a puppy, or crying like a rom-com addict over Watson's bullet wound, and we therefore (secondhand, but secondhand is better than first!) know that he is always and forever full of horse puckey.

What is said about Mary Watson, *nee* Morstan, in the Sherlock Holmes canon? Enough to convince me that she must have been an absolutely extraordinary woman. Let's address the elephant in the room and get ridiculous shipping wars out of the way immediately: no one is saying that John Watson didn't love the "best and wisest man" he'd ever known, or that Holmes wouldn't have gone full Braveheart Mel Gibson if you threatened his army doctor. Sherlock Holmes and John Watson were either brothers-in-arms, or brothers-in-crossed-swords-of-a-certain-type, or something on the spectrum between these paradigms.

This isn't about that. This is about Mary being *awesome*. John "Three Continents" Watson has been around the block, we learn in *The Sign of Four*. Then along comes Mary with some pearls and a mystery, and before you can ejaculate something, John Watson is head over heels. In fact, remember when he developed an epic mancrush for Sherlock Holmes in *A Study in Scarlet*, when he said that the casual reader would

61

doubtless set him down a hopeless busybody over his new consulting detective obsession? Here is what he has to say about Mary Morstan (and John Watson has, I think most will agree, very sound taste regarding the company he keeps): She entered the room:

> [...] with a firm step and an outward composure of manner. She was a blonde young lady, small, dainty, well gloved, and dressed in the most perfect taste. There was, however, a plainness and simplicity about her costume which bore with it a suggestion of limited means. The dress was a sombre grayish beige, untrimmed and unbraided, and she wore a small turban of the same dull hue, relieved only by a suspicion of white feather in the side. Her face had neither regularity of feature nor beauty of complexion, but her expression was sweet and amiable, and her large blue eyes were singularly spiritual and sympathetic. In an experience of women which extends over many nations and three separate continents, I have never looked upon a face which gave a clearer promise of a refined and sensitive nature.

Let's parse this for a second, because of all the people in the canon, John Watson can be counted on to rate inner beauty above outer prickliness, right? He says that she isn't beautiful. (She also isn't "backlit as if caught by surprise, with one hand faintly grasping the doorjamb, the hint of something ripe and J&=RI&EDYFh%@e5r about her lips as she formed a question upon them, appealing to my friend Mr. Sherlock Holmes and wearing a heartbreaking expression of sweet appeal on her angelic and pale yet still cherry-red mouth.")

John Watson is a dude, and John Watson is a good dude, but he is a dude, and he *refuses to objectify her*.

Now, I know you're going to say that she comes to them for help, so she's still a damsel in distress, and yes she's a damsel, and yes she's in distress, but then Watson gets up to leave, because he knows this is probably going to be awkward, and she goes, *halt*:

> To my surprise, the young lady held up her gloved hand to detain me.

'If your friend,' she said, 'would be good enough to stop, he might be of inestimable service to me.'

I relapsed into my chair.

Oh yeah, That One Time When Dr. John H. Watson Who Survived Afghanistan And Even Living With Sherlock Holmes Got "Detained" By This Kinda Terse Lady He Thinks Isn't Beautiful. This is not about a fling. This is not about a conquest. It isn't even about chivalry, not the way he states the case. We only know the canon through Watson's eyes (let's forget "The Lion's Mane" and "The Blanched Soldier" for the moment, shall we?), and he sees in her something formidable and steely, but also something gentle and warm, and he goes on to explicate after they are married that people in trouble flock to Mary "like birds to a lighthouse," one can only assume thanks to both her strength and her kindness.

What does Sherlock Holmes, Reasoning Toaster Oven, think of Mary with his superior man-brain and his mighty deductive powers?

'You are certainly a model client. You have the correct intuition.' […] 'I think she is one of the most charming young ladies I ever met and might have been most useful in such work as we have been doing. She had a decided genius that way …'

I want everyone in the virtual room to perform a simple thought exercise and count the number of times Sherlock Holmes, Consulting Vacuum Cleaner, who *adores* John Watson, ever said Watson had "a decided genius" *about anything at all*. Ever. And when you come up with "making me smarter" and "picking the right stories to tell" as the closest compliments, you will be correct, and Mary will emerge triumphant, and we can all ask her over for whiskey and pie because I don't particularly care for cake. (I'm weird like that.)

Yes, definitely, let's talk about the Other Mary. Well, to be fair, we should make that plural of course … Kelly Reilly does a tremendous turn as Mary Watson, not only tolerating Holmes when necessary (pretty early on) and throwing a drink in his face when necessary (come on, he deserved that one) and being thrown out of a train and still doing super seekrit tasks when necessary (whatever we all thought of Fry's epic casting, we really never saw THAT coming). But she is definitely portrayed as someone Holmes considers an impediment, an objection, a wrench in the proverbial works and not the right kind of wrench, the kind that can help with bolts, which is inconsistent with the Doyle canon in this way:

> Oh, Anstruther would do your work for you. You have been looking a little pale lately. I think that the change would do you good, and you are always so interested in Mr. Sherlock Holmes's cases …

See, that there's Mary, in "The Boscombe Valley Mystery," telling Watson that he looks "a little pale lately," when he thinks about Sherlock Holmes too hard, and needs a strong dose of adventures and service revolvers and mayhem and master blackmailers and devil hounds and the like. Not preventing anything – worthy of being asked along, according to Holmes himself. But content to watch Watson take care of these criminal matters.

What a shame that she was relegated to the backseat so.

Now we can talk about That Other Mary for a bit. Because BBC's Sherlock is badass, almost universally loved telly, and I love them so much, and Mary is difficult, and here is my opinion as to why:

The writers of BBC *Sherlock*, as stated by me before, would like to be thought of as metal. They would like to be so metal that they tour Scandinavia forever, and so stone cold that Alex Lifeson of Rush couldn't say shit to them with a metronome in his damn hand, and so utterly possessing of epic hair that A Flock of Seagulls weep when they behold Moffat and Gatiss. And they are pretty much THAT awesome. This leads them to have to best themselves. This leads them to do things like:

- almost kill Sherlock and John in S1
- actually "kill" Sherlock in S2
- really actually kill kill Sherlock in S3, because what could be more metal than turning it up to 11?
- transform the entire series into a mashup of *James Bond* and *The Ring* in S4

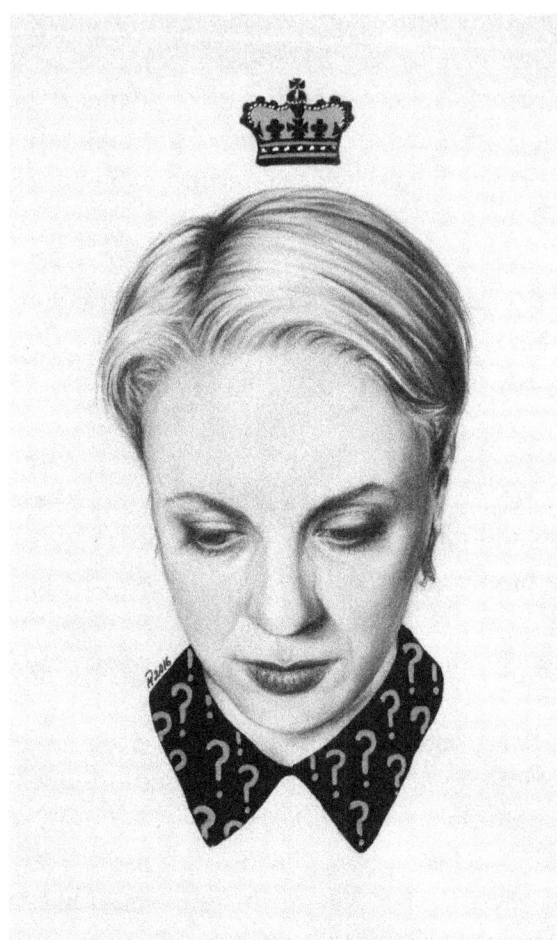

This approach has very little to do with the canonical Mary, at the end of the day. She was a genteel lady of limited means whose shy charm enabled her to help others. Amanda Abbington's Mary is a part time assassin and international superspy who at various points both kills (so metal) and dies for (even more metal) Sherlock Holmes. She's a dry wit, a stone cold killer, a lover of her "Baker Street boys," a mother, a murderer, I dunno, probably also she's in a cult of devil worshippers and then volunteers for Doctors Without Borders in her spare time, let's be honest here, the Everything Has To Be So Metal It Could Open For ACDC approach to storytelling just doesn't really set us up for, er, narrative consistency. There are things to like about this Mary – she bakes bread, is good with dogs, and wants John and Sherlock to have adventures. There are things to dislike as well about the chosen approach – like soaking her character bible in napalm and setting it on fire while "Enter Sandman" plays in the background.

Love her or leave her or something in between. We support you. It's all fine.

In the meanwhile, one could definitely love oneself some canonical Mary. A woman Sherlock Holmes declared "a decided genius" must be pretty spectacular. And yes, 1 am allowing Holmes to define her, but remember ... secondhand evidence is better than firsthand. And Watson agrees with Holmes. And if your two favorite characters both enthusiastically approve of a woman who could have been anything but intelligent and forthright and brave, and turned out to be all three ... well, then I applaud her with all my heart.

Effie Munro and her Daughter Lucy Hebron
by Amy Thomas

"The Yellow Face," along with several other canonical Holmes stories, presents unavoidable difficulties for modern readers. In fact, at a recent convention, my fellow panelist suggested that this story should never have been printed. Before I get into the specifics of why Effie Munro and her daughter are some of the most inspiring women in the *Holmes* canon, I'd like to respectfully address why I disagree with this push for censorship.

First, it's abundantly clear that the story is not politically correct by current standards. It contains problematic terminology and racial characterizations. However, these uncomfortable inclusions accurately reflect a time and place that, as much as they might disturb our sensibilities, did exist at one time. When Warner Brothers shows racially-charged vintage cartoons, they famously include a disclaimer to the effect that while they do not espouse the views of the cartoons, they believe it is harmful to ignore the prejudices that used to exist. As the ubiquitous quote tells us, if we choose to forget history, we're doomed to repeat it. Stories like "The Yellow Face" remind us of how far we've come, but they also remind us of how far we still have to go when it comes to tolerance and respect for human differences.

Second, I am forever willing to defend "The Yellow Face," because, in spite of being a man of his time in his use of terms and stereotypes, Doyle's actual plotting of the story is a rallying cry for acceptance and love that were so far ahead of his time that it boggles the mind. It would be a truly ironic pity for a story that thumbs its nose at the ingrained injustice of the past to be lost to history because we can't see the forest of positives for the problematic trees. That said, I'll move onto the treasure trove of the story itself.

"The Yellow Face" begins in a grim way, with a likable man named Grant Munro seeking Holmes's help to unravel the mystery of why his loving wife, Effie, has suddenly become secretive and given to lying and night-time rendezvous. Munro's story itself reflects Doyle's progressiveness. The man does not abuse, restrict, or otherwise belittle his obviously-troubled wife. He's justifiably concerned by her behavior, but he does not resort to overbearing behavior to get the answer he seeks. He treats her as an equal, which she obviously is.

Effie's behavior appears alarmingly erratic both to the reader and to Holmes, who immediately concocts an explanation for her actions that includes blackmail by her former, supposedly-deceased husband. Things don't look very good for Grant, and they appear even worse for his wife.

That's when one of the most dramatic reversals in the entire canon occurs. A late-night confrontation by Holmes, Watson, and Munro finds none of the sordid details the detective supposed to be true. Instead, Effie is revealed to be the courageous mother of a secret child, desperate to be faithful to her little girl and to her husband. The reason for her secrecy is simple: Her first marriage was interracial, and her child is a reflection of that union. She, like the Victorian reader would have done, assumes that her husband shares the prejudices of his time and will not accept the fact that she is a widow of an interracial marriage or ever be able to love a child who looks so very different from the Victorian ideal.

Effie, while admirably brave and indefatigably strong, is absolutely wrong. Grant Munro tenderly embraces his wife and her child, and the reader is left with the assurance that a new life, as a family, is ahead for the three of them.

Now that we've looked at the story itself, I'll move on to the themes that make Effie and her daughter such amazing women. "The Yellow Face" is a remarkably feminist story, in addition to its progressive racial themes. It's impossible to argue that Doyle wrote it to glorify Holmes's skills, since the detective reads the situation entirely incorrectly and admits as much at the very end. It's also not one that presents a wildly action-packed plot or complicated mystery. It's extremely straightforward in both plot and message. Doyle very obviously wanted to make the statements he made, and he made them very clearly indeed. Let's unpack some of these specifically feminist statements as embodied in the characters of Effie and Lucy.

First, when Grant Munro approaches Holmes, he presents a

picture of his wife that reflects an intelligent, multi-dimensional woman who takes control of her own life and responsibilities. Of Effie, one of his first statements is, "[s]he went out to America when she was young, and lived in the town of Atlanta, where she married." There is no mention here of family connections or obligations. The reader is left to speculate about Effie's reasons for going to America, but it's clear that she's a woman who is ready for adventure and who adapts to her surroundings. Continuing, Grant tells Holmes and Watson that after a yellow fever outbreak claimed the lives of her husband and (he believes) her child, she returned to England and settled on her own with the comfortable living her husband had left behind. Again, we are shown a woman who is not afraid to take the reins of her own life and who is far from desperate to land a man. Her subsequent marriage to Munro is presented as an entirely love-based union, devoid of any damsel-in-distress connotations. In fact, she enters the marriage as the financially-superior partner. As Effie's portrait is first unveiled to us, we are shown, in no uncertain terms, that she is self-actualized, courageous, and mature.

Second, as the story unfolds, Effie's actions prove her strength. Though her behavior seems underhanded at first, in the context of her situation, it

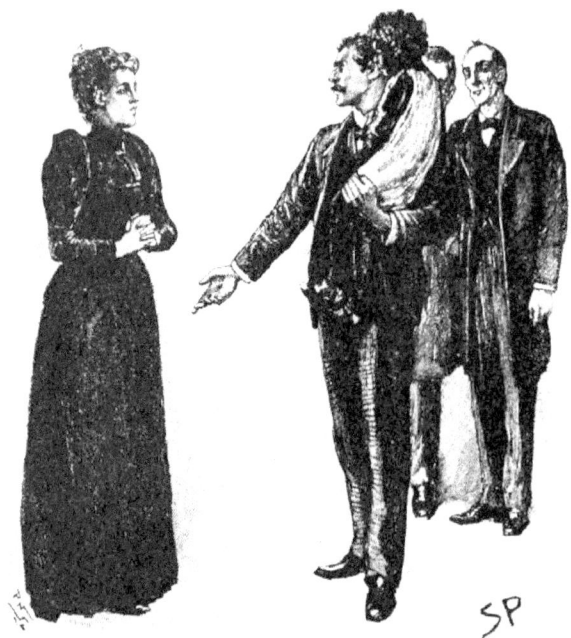

becomes far more admirable. It's not until the end of the story that we discover the truth of her interracial marriage, itself an almost unimaginably brave choice in the context of the American South of her time. Not only does she enter the union, but she also mothers a child of whom she is extremely proud. Her later secrecy has nothing to do with shame about her late husband or beloved child; it's a protective gesture, designed to shelter herself and her daughter from her current husband's rejection. She's a fierce mother, willing to risk a huge amount to care for a child that many people of her time would have refused to acknowledge. Effie's one miscalculation is in her assessment of Grant, who proves to be far more tolerant and admirable than she believed. Like him, the reader can forgive this one thing because her motives are so obviously honorable and extremely understandable.

"The Yellow Face," despite its issues, presents a woman who is smart, brave, decisive, and loyal, unwilling to reject her child in favor of a comfortable life free of others' judgments. Even though she initially fails to realize the extent of Grant's goodness, she is obviously also wise when it comes to her romantic choices, selecting two men to share her life who are honorable and kind beyond the limits of their time. As the child of such a mother, it's hard to imagine Lucy growing up to be anything other than exceptional.

Some may see "The Yellow Face" as the relic of an age best forgotten, but I don't believe Effie Munro or Lucy Hebron would approve.

Sometimes, as readers, we open the pages of history and wade through context and bygone mores to find the diamonds hidden in plain sight among the things that we'd rather not remember.

Effie and her daughter are the creations of a man who operated within the confines of his time and society but also used his pen to joyfully and explosively break those confines wide open to present two women who deserve to be known and understood for years to come. May they never be forgotten in favor of stories we find easier to read.

Mary Russell
by Ardy

Doyle never did tell us what Sherlock Holmes got up to after he retired to a cottage in Sussex, so, much like the Hiatus, that part of his life is a free-for-all for pastiche and fanfiction writers. Whether it turns out that he was Moriarty all along, or slowly succumbs to his addiction, or indeed deteriorates due to dementia – many, many writers have had their wicked way with Holmes-past-fifty.

Laurie R. King is no exception. And so, twenty years ago, Mary Russell entered the scene, fifteen years old, with her nose in a book, wandering in the Sussex Downs to escape her overbearing aunt, and literally fell over Sherlock Holmes. What happened next is the subject of a series of, to date, fifteen novels, two novellas, and a collection of short stories.

While it's not the point of this essay to sell the series to you, it very much is the point of this essay to tell you about some reasons Russell is awesome – seven, to be precise. So I'll get started on that without further ado, and leave you to make up your mind as to whether this is a lady you'd like to hang out with.

She's smart.

When we first meet her, she has her nose in a book because she is studying for the entrance exams at Oxford University. The studying pays off and she eventually graduates with a double degree in theology and chemistry.

From the word go, she is absolutely Holmes' intellectual equal: when she first encounters him, she deduces him as follows:

> 'I'd say the blue spots are a better bet, if you're trying for another hive,' I told him. 'The ones you've only marked with red are probably from Mr Warner's chard. The blue spots are farther away, but they're almost sure to be wild ones.' [...]
> 'How do you come to know of my interests?'
> 'I should have thought it obvious [...] I see paint on your pocket-

handkerchief, and traces on your fingers where you wiped it away. The only reason to mark bees that I can think of is to enable one to follow them to their hive. You are either interested in gathering honey or in the bees themselves, and it is not the time of year to harvest honey. Three months ago we had an unusual cold spell that killed many hives. Therefore I assume that you are tracking these in order to replenish your own stock.'

Sherlock Holmes is not the only one who can play this game, and this is only the first of many examples of Russell's smarts. I could only ever imagine Holmes being interested in someone if they were on the same intellectual level, and Russell exemplifies that. She subsequently proves herself capable at languages and chess as well as her chosen university subjects.

She's badass.

There's a bit of a cliché that you're meant to not be able to deal with the real world if you're a very bookish person, but Russell proves this wrong as well. On their first proper case, Holmes and her get are followed by a pack of vicious hounds. Holmes is about to unleash a drug on them, but Russell faces them down by shouting at them as you would at a gaggle of naughty children.

While this is certainly a showpiece that displays that she has powers she is perhaps unaware of (more on that later), I think it can be argued that the way she deals with her living circumstances is badass in and of itself. Her parents have left her orphaned at a young age, so at the start of the series she is living in a foreign country (she's of American extraction) with an overbearing relative who doesn't like her very much.

Yet instead of grudgingly accepting her situation, she takes active steps to ensure she can get out of there – and I am sure being a young woman at Oxford University in the 1920s was not much of a piece of cake.

She gets to put Holmes in his place.

Oh, does she ever. Holmes is more of a background figure throughout the series, at least in the early volumes. Russell gets to show him his boundaries, but most of all, she gets to call him out on it when he does something unacceptable. One of the early examples in the series is when he deduces her and takes it too far, as he always does, and realizes this. After which she lets him finish and then proceeds to take apart his reasoning and point out the flaws.

This is something I greatly miss from the original stories and most adaptations with the notable exception of *Elementary* (which, in my mind, has more in common with this series than with ACD canon anyway). Here's a bit from *A Monstrous Regiment of Women* when he has knocked her out "for her own good" – a thing that I think is never okay, and Russell has the same opinion:

> I pulled back, and I hit him—nothing fancy, just a good, traditional, lady's open-handed slap that had all the muscles of my arm behind it. It rattled his teeth and nearly sent him back into the river. I glared furiously at him.
> 'Never, never do that again!'
> 'Russell! I did not—'
> 'Knock me out and leave me behind—Holmes, how could you?'
> 'There was no time for a discussion,' he pointed out.
> 'That is no excuse,' I said illogically. 'Never even think of doing something like that again!'

Holmes has had a punch in the face about his arsehole tendencies coming since about 1894, but since Watson never quite stepped up to the challenge (at least not until the BBC adaptation came along), I'm glad *someone* got there.

She gets to travel.

Don't get me wrong, I love London and I love the ACD stories, but the furthest Holmes and Watson ever go from London is to other parts of

England. Russell and Holmes's adventures take them to Dartmoor (obligatory stop for any pastiche series), Palestine, America, India, Portugal, Morocco, and Japan. She adapts to all manner of different social customs and languages with ease (though she relies on a disguise once). She also gets to confront people's hang-ups about women and her relationship with Holmes, and because she's younger she gets to do stuff that Holmes isn't able to do.

Her story continues after the marriage.

It's not a spoiler to say that Russell and Holmes get married at the end of the second book, because it's the basis of the conceit of the rest of the series. I'm not going to spend much ink on Mary Sue debates here, but I feel compelled to point out that I really don't know that many female characters whose stories continue after they get married to whoever it was the plot was setting them up with. For these two, I feel the marriage is more like a socially acceptable excuse from the writer to keep them around each other so that the series can continue. Also, the way it happens at the end of *A Monstrous Regiment of Women*, right after the showdown of the case and after Russell has had to fish Holmes out of the water and given him a decent box on the ears for underestimating her, is one of my favourite marriage proposals in literature. It's too long to quote but you can find it online.

She grows over the course of the series.

Russell is fifteen when the series starts, but as it continues she grows from an awkward teenager into a capable young woman. She's a feminist, she gets involved with people on the margins of society despite being a young lady of means, she gets to confronts the ghosts of her own and Holmes' past, and she gets to develop security in herself. It's been a pleasure getting through my teens and twenties alongside her, and I'm happy she's still around now I've hit thirty. (She hasn't yet, the lucky sod.)

She's one of not very many "female Watsons" I know of.

Watson is everyman, for sure, and if you ask BSB Lyndsay whose shoes she'd want to walk in, it would be Watson's. In the canon, definitely, but in the realm of pastiche, I'd slip into Russell's shoes at any time, although, as mentioned before, Joan Watson from *Elementary* is some serious competition. They get to hang out with Holmes, but they also get to do their own thing. And every so often, it's nice to have a character to inhabit and walk alongside that you don't have to cross gender divides for.

I hope we get to read a few more of Russell and Holmes' adventures before the author decides she's had enough of them.

Mrs. Ronder
by Ro Gorczyca

The tales of Sherlock Holmes are pretty unique in the fact that between each story, there is often no consistent genre. Many of the stories are mysteries, from which we get the idea of Holmes as a great detective. On par with that is the number of stories that are basically adventures; *The Adventures of Sherlock Holmes* is an accurate name for that reason. But there are some stories that not only stand out in their genre, but also stand out in the fact that they are overlooked and often not remembered as clearly as some of the more standout titles in the collection.

One of those stories is the account of "The Adventure of the Veiled Lodger"; — Watson's transcription of how he and Holmes listened to Mrs. Ronder's story, and the search for the truth that Holmes had been on for years. Although it shares the title of "adventure" with many more of Watson's tales, the story is mostly a personal account from of Mrs. Ronder's life, from in which we learn of the villainy that had plagued her in her younger years, and the murder with which she had been involved, resulting in her current state of an unfair existence.

The story, in brief, is the account of her husband. Mr. Ronder was an angry and abusive man, as well as a showman, who owned a lion which he used for part of his greatest act. Many members of his company left because of his character. Mrs. Ronder and Leonardo, a strong man, were soon the only two members keeping the show alive, and eventually became lovers. After a very vicious attack on Mrs. Ronder from her husband, Leonardo and Mrs. Ronder decided that he must die.

Mrs. Ronder and her husband went to feed the lion one night and Leonardo hit Mr. Ronder on the head with a club fashioned to look like lion's claws. Mrs. Ronder then let the lion out of its cage, to make the attack seem more authentic, but the animal turned on her and severely wounded her face. Instead of attacking the lion and protecting the woman he loved, Leonardo fled.

On the surface, there are two ways to look at this story. Mrs.

Ronder was with an abusive husband, and the fact that he was so vile (and was not the man she loved) was very much the reason for his death. But one might also say that for whatever wrongs Mrs. Ronder was subjected to at his hands, her husband still did not deserve to be killed. Her story is one of interest because of the moral problem (like many in Watson's writings) that it presents.

However, as a Holmes story, we can judge her by Holmes's standards, under which he fully understands and does not turn Mrs. Ronder over to the police.

In all this, we learn many things about Mrs. Ronder in a few short pages. Firstly, although going to anyone about the truth of the event would mean Mrs. Ronder would have been in danger of arrest, that was not her main reason for keeping silent at the time and the years that followed. She thought instead of Leonardo, despite his betrayal. "I know that he was a worthless being, and yet I would not have his destruction upon my conscience," she says, insisting that Leonardo's fate had depended on her keeping quiet.

Secondly, we can see the truth in Holmes's summary of her life; as he says "[t]he example of patient suffering is in itself the most precious of all lessons to an impatient world." Mrs. Ronder had spent a long time with her beast of a husband, and still continued on working with him and the others in the show every day. She also spent a while long time clinging to her love for Leonardo while still married to her husband and being subjected to Ronder's "revenge in his own way by torturing [her] more than ever." And in her later years, Mrs. Ronder had hung onto life, even in the terrible form that she experienced it, hiding up in her lodgings and shielding her injured face from the world.

And finally, what we learn ties together these aspects and may be the most important characteristic: her bravery. She was brave to hold out in a life with her husband, and to take action against him. She was also brave to protect Leonardo, even though telling her story may have meant more catharsis for her and a kind of justice for him abandoning her. She was also quite brave to exist in life afterward for as long as she was planning to. Mrs. Ronder lived in her lodgings, avoiding the world. She claims to not care about what

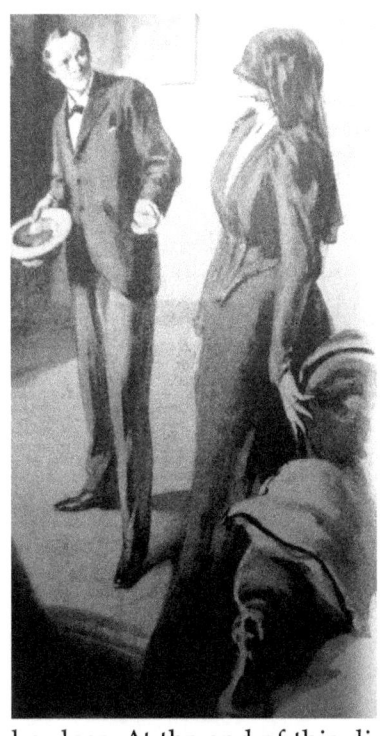

will happen to her – "What could be more dreadful than my actual life?" – and shows Holmes her scarred face, asking if he would bear to live in such a state.

Lastly, her bravery shows in a way that even Holmes has to commend. As we find out, the final twist of Mrs. Ronder's tale is not, as she tells her landlady, that she is growing ill, dying, and therefore wants the truth to be told, but that she is planning to kill herself. After the telling of her story, Mrs. Ronder says with a certain finality: "Yes, the case is closed," causing Holmes to advise her that her life is still worth living, because others would suffer from her loss. At the end of this discussion, Mrs. Ronder doesn't seem to believe Holmes, or want to take his advice and live. However, two days later Holmes receives a note in the post, and with it a bottle of prussic acid, from Mrs. Ronder. She has reconsidered – "the brave woman," Holmes calls her.

For some, it might seem like a triumph of Holmes, to talk her out of suicide. But truly, Mrs. Ronder deserves all the credit – for finding the courage and making the choice to live.

Ettie Shafter
by Maria Fleischhack

One lady from the *Sherlock Holmes* stories is one who is often overlooked, rarely discussed and almost never featured in adaptations: Ettie Shafter, a young woman living with her father Jacob in Vermissa Valley, Pennsylvania. She is one of the tragic female characters in the canon, characterized by her tolerance and open-mindedness, by her will to fight for herself and her kin, and to love unconditionally.

Arthur Conan Doyle published his final *Sherlock Holmes* novel *The Valley of Fear* in 1915. Just as he does with the first two novels, Doyle creates a case which Holmes has to solve and then sets the background story abroad. In this case, the story is that of a secret agent by the name of John Douglas (The artist formerly known as John McMurdo aka. Birdy Edwards) from Chicago, who infiltrates the Ancient Order of Freemen, the "The Scowrers", Lodge 341, Vermissa Valley, Pennsylvania. The Scowrers tyrannize Vermissa Valley, and those who work in the mines there live in constant fear of the gang. The secret agent slips into the role of a freemason and takes on the dangerous task of exposing the terrible doings of the Scowrers.

McMurdo looks for a place to lodge in the valley and meets Ettie Shafter, who is the daughter of a German immigrant, Jacob Shafter. The young woman appears like a beacon of light in the dark and dangerous place:

> [The door] was opened at once by someone very different from what he had expected. It was a woman, young and singularly beautiful. She was of the German type, blonde and fair-haired, with the piquant contrast of a pair of beautiful dark eyes with which she surveyed the stranger with surprise and a pleasing embarrassment which brought a wave of colour over her pale face. Framed in the bright light of the open doorway, it seemed to McMurdo that he had never seen a more beautiful picture; the more attractive for its contrast with the sordid and gloomy surroundings. A lovely violet growing upon one of those black slag-heaps of the mines would not have seemed more surprising. So entranced was he that he stood

staring without a word, and it was she who broke the silence.

McMurdo, who is used to solving murder cases and who has seen the worst in men, is speechless when confronted with the woman. Before she has even said a word, he is quite clearly in love with her. Doyle compares her to a violet, a name he used for two rather lovely independent women in the canon stories. All of this is of course told from a man's perspective, and she hasn't spoken yet.

However, when she speaks, we realize that she is quite a special young lady.

> 'I thought it was father,' said she with a pleasing little touch of a German accent. […] 'Come right in, sir,' she said. 'I'm Miss Ettie Shafter, Mr. Shafter's daughter. My mother's dead, and I run the house. You can sit down by the stove in the front room until father comes along – Ah, here he is! So you can fix things with him right away.'

She lives in a town in which everyone is scared all the time, and, as we learn later, she is promised to one of the Scowrers. Yet she trusts this stranger entirely. It is both a very stupid and a very smart move.

McMurdo is offered a place to stay and generally treated very well by Jacob until he admits to belonging to a lodge. Jacob becomes immediately hostile, whereas Ettie feels that he doesn't belong to them, making excuses that other masonic lodges are interested in peace and kindness. She begs McMurdo not to get involved with the Scowrers.

Her pleading gains more justification when McMurdo learns that she is involved with Baldwin, one of the most brutal members of the gang. It's quite obvious that she doesn't love or even like him, but that she is trying to keep the peace by not rejecting him. The appearance of McMurdo and his obvious interest in her leads to jealousy and an even more explosive climate in the valley.

One of the underlying plotlines in the story, which focuses on the gang and their evil deeds, is Ettie's role in the conflict. The secret agent establishes himself quickly in the lodge and becomes something of a favorite of the leader, Jack McGinty. Knowing that it will make things more complicated, McMurdo lays claim on Ettie, which drives Baldwin into blind hatred and suspicion against both the new man in town and the lady.

While the storyline seems to apply the damsel in distress trope, Ettie is the one who suggests to run away with McMurdo. Her plan is to take the man she feels is a better person than he lets on away from danger, and to move herself and her father out of the "valley of fear."

While her wish is eventually and dramatically fulfilled, and they flee overnight after McMurdo proves the murderous intentions of the gang, it appears that Ettie is as concerned about him as she is about her own family.

As a character, she seems quite independent and intelligent, and sees McMurdo for what he is. Her ticket out of hell.

She runs her father's guest house, she consciously keeps the most violent men of the gang close to her in order to ensure her personal safety, and she trusts a person who seems to have trouble trusting himself.

At one point, Ettie finds McMurdo writing a letter and he reacts by violently grabbing and choking her – until he realizes who he is choking. Ettie suspects that he is writing to another woman. Since he cannot blow his own cover and tell her that he is reporting back to Chicago, he can only ask for her trust … and despite the treatment she experienced, she decides to trust him after all. It's a highly problematic scene, and the fact that McMurdo/Edwards/Douglas is lying to her while she blindly trusts him definitely dampens the reader's appreciation of his character.

However, I find Ettie's trust not only naïve, but also admirable. She is an immigrant who found that her new life in the land of infinite possibilities has become a nightmare. McMurdo, despite his violent outbreak, seems the safer option than Baldwin, who is highly abusive.

In an unsafe environment, the natural consequence would be suspicion and hate, yet Ettie chooses to put her trust in a stranger and her trust is rewarded. They flee the valley and get married in Chicago. Sadly, she doesn't live for long, and her death casts a dark shadow over Douglas's life.

What is striking about her is that she is a constant positive (if naïve) character in the middle of this often disturbing story. Even though she has reason to believe that the man she loves is writing to other women, she remains true to him and finds a way out of her dreadful situation – even if it is only for a few short years.

Her external and internal beauty is so striking that the UK publication changed her nationality from German to Swedish, owing to the fact that England was at war with Germany when the story was published. She was simply too positive for a German character at that time, even if she represents one of many thousand German immigrants in the United States at the beginning of the century.

I find the character of Ettie Shafter very interesting and I would like to see her explored in adaptations and pastiches. She is mostly ignored (as is the novel) in terms of adaptations. Norma Green's animated Sherlock Holmes adaptation of *The Valley of Fear* (1983), for instance, completely cuts her out of the story.

However, one adaptation gives her much more screen time than the novel offers. In *The Triumph of Sherlock Holmes* from 1935, Ettie appears not only in Vernissa Valley, where she is presented as quite a strong young woman, but is allowed to remain alive and follow her husband to England, where she meets Holmes and Watson during their investigations. The adaptation gives Ettie a chance which Doyle didn't give her, and I must say that I appreciate this change very much.

Violet Smith

by Melinda Caric

I'll get to Violet in a minute, but first: let's talk about women on bicycles.

As an avid cyclist myself, I think that focusing on Miss Smith's chosen form of transportation is a good way to reveal a bit more about the workings of her character. People usually don't give the subject a second thought: it's a form of transport, of exercise, and of recreation, as well as being a thing that both sexes enjoy and participate in equally. But it hasn't always been this way. When the modern bicycle (then called a 'safety bicycle') with a chain drive was first invented by John Kemp Starley, it was a huge technological advancement over the dangerous and cumbersome penny-farthing, and people began to take up cycling as a hobby en masse. And by people, I mean men.

The women who first worked up the courage to try cycling were, predictably enough, publicly shamed and ridiculed. Cycling required improper posture for a lady, strenuous exercise while wearing long skirts and a corset which resulted in dangerous conditions, and it also carried the very real possibility of injury: no lady of the day would willingly be seen with a bruise on her that might mean she had been moving around or doing something equally unladylike.

But far worse than all of the above was that riding a bicycle required the rider to put her ladybits on a saddle (oh! the scandal!) with her legs on either side of the top tube (*faints*). There were naturally some side saddle options made available, but they were largely unstable and overly complicated. To have women ride bicycles the way they were meant to be ridden simply wouldn't do. If women sat astride anything at all it would create a nation of hysterical nymphomaniacs, not to mention it would call attention to their legs. In the Victorian era, to be a woman and to have legs was just considered rude.

As we are all aware, a glimpse of a woman's ankle would be enough to incite riots and ruin her family's good name, so a device called Cherry's Screen was invented to hide those gams from view so she'd look like less of a Slutty McHobag.

Keep in mind that our drama takes place in the year 1895, and attitudes towards women on bicycles had not yet shifted – the safety bicycle was only introduced in 1887, which means that all of the above issues regarding women on bicycles were still very much a part of public perception at the time of our story.

Now with that bit of historical context out of the way, I think we can view Violet Smith with a more enlightened perspective than before. The fact that she rides a bicycle at all is a very clear indicator that she is not a woman to be trifled with. She knows what she wants, doesn't give a damn what others think about it, and will pursue her goals with determination and single-mindedness. The fact that she had the wits to consult with Holmes at all once she found herself in trouble proves that she knows

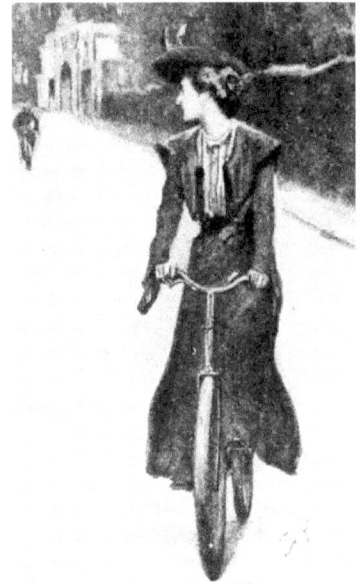

how to find the right tool for the job. And his initial cold reception didn't phase her one bit: "It was vain to urge that his time was already fully occupied, for the young lady had come with the determination to tell her story, and it was evident that nothing short of force could get her out of the room until she had done so." Translation: Oh, I'm sorry, is my being here inconvenient to you? Too bad, dork, you're going to listen to me anyway. But her admirable qualities don't end there. When Holmes pulls out his bicycling deduction, she's quick enough to follow his line of reasoning and knows exactly

how he came to that conclusion. She's young, beautiful, tall, graceful, queenly, fit, and observant, with a spiritual face and a presumably hot fiancée. Is there anything this woman cannot do?

Oh, and let's not forget – while she believes herself to be alone and at her most vulnerable, she races forward on her bike like the Gino Bartali of her day to take on her own stalker. This is a move so gutsy it cannot be overemphasized. Here is a woman being tormented by a mysterious and unwanted attendant whose intentions are unknown, and while she is on a very lonely stretch of road chooses to confront her fears and her pursuer rather than allow someone to psychologically bully her. For that single action alone I think she can be regarded as one of the most courageous women in the canon.

In 1896 suffragette Susan B. Anthony said "[l]et me tell you what I think of bicycling. I think it has done more to emancipate women than any single other thing in the world. It gives women a feeling of freedom and self-reliance. I stand and rejoice every time I see a woman ride by on a wheel, the picture of free, untrammeled womanhood." Violet Smith herself is the very picture of free, untrammeled womanhood. I couldn't have said it any better myself.

Beryl Stapleton
by Ashley D. Polasek

If I were to ask you to list the three canonical women who have appeared on screen most frequently, I bet you'd get two out of three. "Mrs. Hudson!" you might cry first, and you'd be right; Mrs. H. always seems on hand, regardless of the adventure and far outnumbers any other woman for appearances on screen. "Irene Adler!" you'd no doubt add, and that's likely true, as she's the go-to female foil for Holmes and is adapted into far more tales than her one canonical appearance. For the third, you're probably tempted to say Mary Morstan, but, unlike Irene, she rarely turns up outside the context of *The Sign of Four*, and a glance at Sherlockian filmography (a more complete one than IMDb presents) indicates that *Sign* is the second most adapted tale – outnumbered as much as four times by film and television versions of that most beloved of stories, *The Hound of the Baskervilles*. The woman at the center of *Hound*, then, earns the third spot on our list: Beryl Stapleton.

Like Mrs. Hudson, Irene Adler, and Mary Morstan, Beryl Stapleton has turned up enough times that her role in the story, her personality, her behavior, and even her appearance, do not always correspond to the canonical *Hound*, but if we're going to get a clear picture of this cunning and mercurial woman, we should start there.

Beryl makes her first appearance nearly half way through *Hound*, when, thinking Watson is Sir Henry Baskerville, she appears on the moor to warn him of the dangers he faces if he doesn't immediately return to London. Watson, with ever the eye for a pretty face, describes her as "a beauty … of the most uncommon type." She is "darker than any brunette whom I have seen in England – slim, elegant, and tall" with a "proud finely cut face," "sensitive mouth," and "beautiful, dark, eager eyes." "With her perfect figure and elegant dress," he adds, "she was, indeed, a strange apparition upon a lonely moorland path." Steady, Watson. She's totally going to be a love interest, but not yours. Keep it together.

Their little tête-à-tête is cut short by the return of Jack Stapleton, Beryl's "brother" (wink-wink), but one more curious thing happens. Stapleton offers this offhand remark: "And yet we manage to make ourselves fairly happy, do we not, Beryl?" to which she replies: "Quite happy." Watson, who may be slightly more observant than we give him credit for, poor chap, notes that "there was no ring of conviction in her words." This is Beryl in a nutshell: she is a woman trapped, a woman in conflict, a woman, in short, who wants to do the right thing, but is daily in fear for her life. Beryl Stapleton is clever, and she has the strength and will of ten hell hounds.

Here's the thing about Beryl Stapleton: she has it rough. She married a suave crook in her native Costa Rica (insert obligatory apology for ACD's casual and consistent racism toward Latinas, and for filmmakers who often feel the need to recast her as a blonde haired, blue eyed English rose) and followed him through a series of illegal operations. Was she part of his nefarious plots? Probably. We learn later that he abuses her both emotionally and physically, though, so it's hard to judge her for that – she'd have found little sympathy from the authorities as a foreigner and an abused married woman in 1889; she didn't have many options. Once settled on the moor, she is forced to pretend to be her husband's sister, which means Stapleton essentially planned to pimp her out to a series of Baskervilles in order to get his hands on the manor, title, and fortune. As Watson notes, Stapleton is a two ton pile of hound shit. (I am paraphrasing slightly.)

Although she is stuck pretending to be the unmarried Miss Beryl Stapleton, to her credit, she draws the line at luring kind old men to their certain deaths, and refuses to throw herself at Sir Charles. She also does what she can to warn off Sir Henry – going right to the edge of mortal danger. On the one hand, she doesn't want to be complicit in murder. On the other, she loves her husband and also fears him ("they are by no means incompatible emotions," Holmes notes). She lives on the razor's edge, caring for Sir Henry, enduring savage beatings from Stapleton, and deceiving everyone on every side to stay alive and keep her dignity. She plays a dangerous game. In the end, she turns on her murderous husband, and Holmes concedes a detail that we often forget: if the detective and the doctor had not solved the mystery when they had, Beryl, who had all the information from the start, would have gone to the police in any case. Holmes and Watson who?

I mentioned that Beryl has appeared on screen enough to grow beyond the story that Conan Doyle wrote for her. Her role has been fundamentally different in several versions of *Hound*, and the role she plays often defines the whole character of the adaptation, which speaks to her place as a lynchpin in the most popular Sherlock Holmes story. I'll spare you the hours it would take to rehash every version and just offer three.

In 1939's *Hound*, starring Basil Rathbone, Beryl was stripped of her backstory – she really was Stapleton's sister. This let the romance she had with Sir Henry pass the censors (the Hayes Code prohibited films from suggesting that any good, like, say, marrying the gorgeous baronet and gaining happiness, wealth, and title, could come from adultery. Obviously married women in abusive relationships with murderous crooks must stay that way because Morality). This Beryl, who presumably got to live happily ever after, may hold the honor of being the only woman in any role ever to be billed above both Holmes and Watson in a Sherlock Holmes movie. Like I said: Holmes and Watson who?

Hammer's marvelous B-movie from 1959 re-imagines Beryl completely. She is restored to her Spanish roots, transformed into Stapleton's daughter, and is renamed Cecile for good measure. She appears young, wild, barefoot, and boobilicious, and although this film is totally enjoyable anyhow, it's worth watching just to see her charm Christopher Lee's basso profundo clean off, and leave him silent and glassy-eyed. (Christopher Lee snogging, anyone? Just me? Ok.) Of course, in becoming Stapleton's daughter, she also becomes a Baskerville, not an unwitting and misused accomplice, but the mastermind behind the plan to kill both Sir Charles and Sir Henry. Instead of a fairytale romance, she gets a slurping trip to the bottom of the Grimpen Mire, but damn did she have some agency before she went.

1959 was not the only year Miss Stapleton met a bad end. There is a bit of intra-Babe conflict regarding the made-for-TV version of *Hound* from 2002 starring Richard Roxburgh. (And by intra-Babe conflict I mean that Lyndsay and I once stayed up until silly o'clock drinking rum and debating its relative merits: she despises it almost as much as Rupert Everett's eyebrows; it's one of my favorites.) I think it handles the climax in a more thrilling way than any other. This climax includes Richard E. Grant's impeccably slimy Stapleton announcing "I have no wife" with chilling calm, several times over, as Holmes presents his evidence and Watson frantically searches the house for Beryl. Watson finally finds her, beaten and hanged in an outbuilding. In his blind Watsonian rage, he rushes in and attempts to kill Stapleton, which precipitates the rest of the action. Even in death, Beryl is the center of the action.

Sometimes villain, sometimes victim, Beryl Stapleton is one of the most complex women in the *Sherlock Holmes* canon. She drives Sir Henry wild, drives Stapleton to distraction, and above all, drives the plot no matter what part she's given to play in it. So next time you're making a catalogue of canonical ladies, make sure that Beryl Stapleton is near the top. Because you sure as hell don't want to be on her bad side.

Mrs. St. Clair
by Ashley D. Polasek

"You would have done better to have trusted your wife," says Sherlock Holmes to an abashed and exposed Neville St. Clair at the conclusion of "The Man with the Twisted Lip." Isn't that so often the case? Mrs. Neville St. Clair is one of the many women in the canon who is never given a name of her own (though let's face it, it's probably Violet or Mary. Probably Violet). This lack of identifier should not be mistaken for lack of identity. Nor should it suggest a lack of character or of purpose. Mrs. St. Clair instigates the action, knowingly leads the police and Holmes to vital clues, and maintains the base of operations during the case.

While many canonical cases revolve around women, Mrs. St. Clair is at the center of this one without being either a victim or a villain. She is an everywoman: a devoted wife and a loving mother. And like so many wives and mothers – certainly mine, and perhaps yours as well – she is a rock, and expert manager of people and situations, and has a felicity for cutting through bullshit.

The case is triggered when Mrs. (Violet or Mary) St. Clair sees her husband flailing out of the upper window of the sort of establishment that makes other seedy rat-infested rookeries look like cozy tea shops. What does she do? She makes instant note of the fact that Neville is not wearing a collar and tie, because details matter, registers that he seems to be in distress, and immediately rushes into this hideous den of vice to rescue him. She tries to muscle her way past the sinister toughs blocking the stairway, and she has to be carried out bodily before she gives up and fetches the police. There is no strength like the strength of a woman when her family is threatened.

Holmes spends a long cab ride to the St. Clairs' home in Kent musing to Watson over how sorry he is not to have good news for his client (for, presumably, just as she engaged the police, Mrs. St. Clair enlisted Holmes), and how worried she is for her husband. The reader might therefore expect a frail, weeping thing to greet Holmes and Watson, but instead, we get a different sight altogether: "She stood with her figure outlined against the flood of light, one hand upon the door, one half raised in her eagerness, her body slightly bent, her head and face protruded, with eager eyes and parted lips, a standing question." Following an introduction to Watson and a brief exchange with Holmes, she ushers the men into her house and proceeds to grill the detective in the most satisfyingly forthright manner:

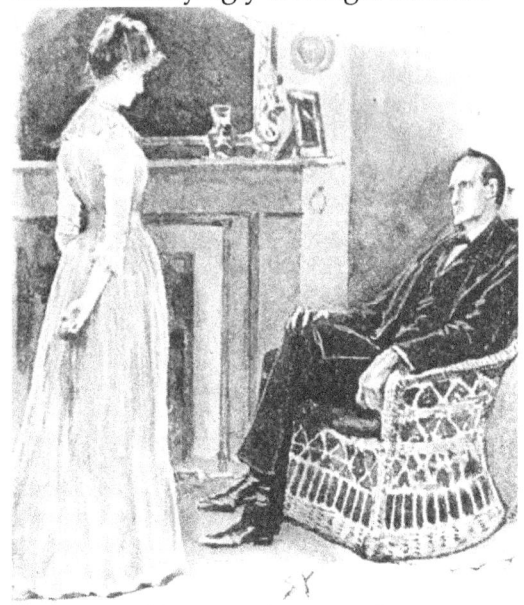

"Now, Mr. Sherlock Holmes … I should very much like to ask you one or two plain questions, to which I beg that you will give a plain answer. … Do not trouble about my feelings. I am not hysterical, nor given to fainting. I simply wish to hear your real, real opinion."

While she grills Holmes, she is "standing upon the rug and looking keenly down at him as he leaned back in a basket chair." As a personal confession, every time I read this I imagine my own mum interrogating a different version of Holmes. And every time, every version cowers and must collect himself before he answers.

There is one other unique quality of Mrs. St. Clair: while her husband is missing, she allows two bachelors to stay in her house with her. Several commentators have posited that she was having a dalliance with Holmes (who was meant to be staying with her on his own), and others have suggested she had designs on him that he was relieved to escape through Watson's serendipitous presence. For my part, I think she didn't care if her reputation was ruined if it meant the safe return of her husband, and was simply happy to offer whatever help Holmes requested; she's a practical woman. The long and the short of it is that Mrs. St. Clair is not to be trifled with, and quite frankly, if she ever does learn the truth of his activities from her husband, I wouldn't trade places with him for all the coppers Hugh Boone ever collected.

Helen Stoner
by Taylor Blumenberg

I want to talk about one of the more overlooked Sherlockian ladies: Miss Helen Stoner.

Miss Stoner is featured quite prominently as the client in "The Adventure of the Speckled Band," a story that even Doyle himself called his favorite. Miss Stoner approaches Holmes following the unsettling request from her stepfather, Dr. Roylott, that she should move from her bedroom into another room whilst work is done on her own chambers. This may not be that unsettling a request were it not for the fact that the room she is being moved into is the very room in which her twin sister Julia died just before her wedding, leaving behind only the baffling final words of "[t]he band! The speckled band!"

Miss Stoner may not seem particularly remarkable – she is a spinster in her 30's still living with her father, though newly engaged to be married – but her strength of character lies within the bravery and brightness she displays throughout the story. Dr. Roylott is a particularly ill-tempered man and certainly not someone to be trifled with, as is shown when he bends Holmes's fireplace poker out of shape with his bare hands. In spite of his violent demeanor Miss Stoner still seeks Holmes's advice in the matter. Knowing full well that her stepfather will not approve and may likely follow her, Helen veils herself and takes an early morning train into the city. While she is motivated by her fear of what may happen to her she certainly shows great bravery in going against a man at whose hand, as Holmes observes during her brief visit to 221B, she has been, "cruelly used." It is even mentioned in the story that Miss Stoner shows signs of physical abuse, bearing the marks of Roylott's fingers as vivid red spots upon her wrist. However, despite this domestic violence Helen still manages to seek Holmes's council.

Also, allow me to mention that the residence Miss Stoner lives at, Stoke Moran, is home to several exotic pets, specifically a cheetah and a baboon. These animals belong to Dr. Roylott and have free run of the grounds. One can't help but feel that it would take a certain kind of bravery to take a turn around the garden knowing that there was a very real chance you may encounter a cheetah. It only makes sense that she was ready to marry and escape Stoke Moran and the terrifying creatures, human and otherwise, that populated its grounds.

The physical description of Miss Stoner which is provided certainly paints a picture of a woman who is haunted by the death of her sister and living in a state of fear. Watson remarks that Helen has "restless, frightened eyes" and compares her to a "hunted animal." It is also mentioned that Helen's hair has "premature grey", a physical feature which is no doubt the result of the stressful life she lives, haunted by her sister's death and tormented by her abusive father.

She is also quite clever, as illustrated by the fact that Miss Stoner comes to Holmes, not only with the story of her sister's death, but with a theory on what her last words may have meant. She suspects that the gypsies may have murdered her sister and that the "speckled band" may be a reference either to the gypsies themselves, as a band of people, or to the spotted handkerchiefs they wear. While this theory is, of course, proved wrong by Holmes, it speaks well of Helen's intelligence and curiosity that she has set the puzzle out for her own mind before approaching the detective with her suspicions.

The character of Helen Stoner also carries an interesting distinction in that she is actually known by another name in a different adaptation of the story. In 1910 Doyle, inspired by the success of William Gillette's portrayal of Holmes on stage, adapted the original into a stage play called *The Stonor Case*. In this version of the story, amongst other minor changes, the character of Helen Stoner is called Enid Stonor and is the stepdaughter of Dr. Grimsesby Rylott. It is quite interesting to see such a change as it allows one to look into Doyle's writing process in a way, allowing us to watch the evolution of the tale and giving a

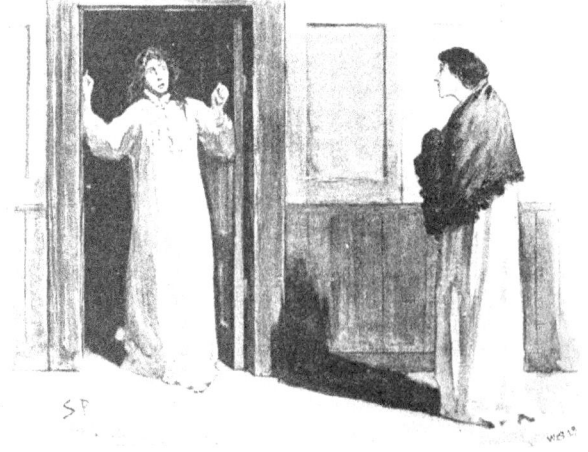

character with a one off appearance a chance at character development.

Helen Stoner is an often overlooked character, one who may initially seem to be a cookie cutter damsel in distress, but the way in which she handles her tribulations lends much to the character, creating another rather strong female presence in the Sherlockian canon.

Mary Sutherland
by Elinor Gray

Miss Mary Sutherland of No. 31 Lyon Place, Camberwell, is a wronged woman, and not just by her scumbag stepfather. Sherlock Holmes, master of his craft and generally-reliable hero figure, makes a grave error in the case of Mary Sutherland; one of the worst mistakes in his published career.

Miss Sutherland arrives on the stoop of 221 Baker Street in a confused hurry: she needs to consult Holmes, but she isn't certain what he can do for her yet. Holmes and Watson spot her from the window, and Holmes makes his famous remark about "oscillation upon the pavement" being suggestive of "an *affaire du coeur*."

Watson does not do the lady justice either, from the start. He makes attempts upon her arrival to portray her as comical, calling her "large" and "loom[ing] … like a full-sailed merchantman" as she enters

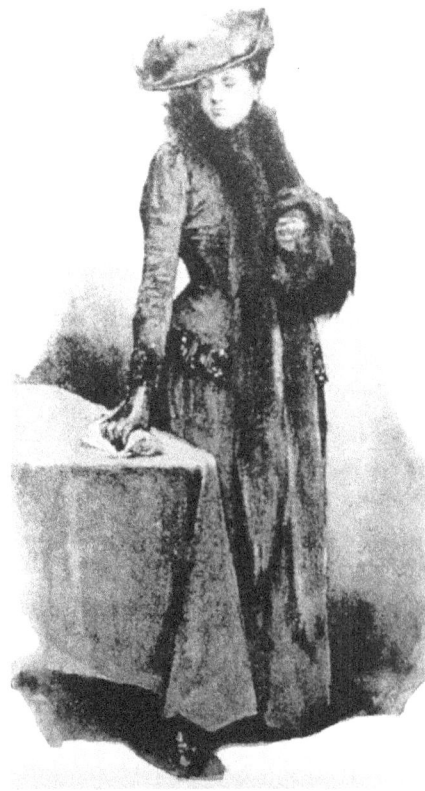

the apartment. He describes her "broad, good-humoured" face and almost immediately follows that up by calling her "vacuous." Later, he says, "there was something noble in the simple faith of our visitor which compelled our respect." Not very powerfully, it seems.

Which is a shame, really, because she is a woman worthy of their respect. She is the kind of woman many women want to be: independent and resourceful with some potential for financial stability in her own right, kind and amiable, as well as innocent and optimistic enough to fall in love. She sees good in the world where there is none, and she would have had enough money to take advantage of it if she were not cruelly tricked by her mother and step-father. Miss Sutherland makes claims to an income of "a hundred a year" from the interest on stock left to her by an uncle in New Zealand, which is drawn upon by her parents while she lives with them; on top of that, she makes tuppence a page type-writing, up to twenty pages a day. The woman is self-employed and good at it, despite her literal short-sightedness. Miss Sutherland, as a woman Watson describes as "fairly well-to-do in a vulgar, comfortable, easy-going way," is living her best life. All she wants now is to be loved.

After she departs Baker Street, Holmes observes that their visitor was "of a good, amiable disposition, but affectionate and warm-hearted in her ways," and says, "it was evident that with her fair personal advantages, and her little income, she would not be allowed to remain single long." Sweet, kind, and moderately wealthy: she should have her pick of nice men. Instead she gets her creepy, greedy step-father, Mr. Windibank, in a false beard.

Her independent-mindedness, which should be her third admirable feature after her money and her disposition, is what puts her in the path of trouble. Wishing only to reconnect with people she knew when her father was alive, she defies her step-father's demands that she and her mother "never … go anywhere" and attends the gasfitters' ball, "for what right had [Windibank] to prevent?" She has a lovely dress to wear, and friends to see, and she just wants to have a nice time. Windibank, counting on this act of defiance, springs his trap and woos her in tinted glasses. One wonders if they have had dust-ups before, in which Windibank forbid something and Mary Sutherland did it anyway. How else could he have expected her to attend (disregard, for the moment, her mother's complicit involvement and pushy enthusiasm)? If she were timid or retiring, she would not have insisted on going to the ball or agreed to continue to see well-dressed, whispery Hosmer Angel behind her stepfather's back.

All of these qualities in a woman ought to have caught Sherlock Holmes's attention, who has a fondness for independent ladies with jobs and prospects. He certainly recognized the good nature of the lady, and knew that she was being wronged. He tells her to forget Hosmer

Angel, that he is certain she will never see him again. He offered to whip Windibank with his riding crop, being so incensed by the notion of this dreadful plan. But then, for no discernible reason, he laughs to himself and goes to smoke his pipe, having no intention of telling his client the truth of the matter.

"If I tell her she will not believe me," he says. To his credit, she has already declared, "I shall be true to Hosmer. He shall find me ready when he comes back," but as a private detective (*not* a member of the official force, as he is quick to remind us, and the arbiter of his own form of justice) he has a duty to his client to give them enough of the facts to make an informed decision. "There is danger for him who taketh the tiger cub," Holmes quotes, "and danger also for whoso snatches a delusion from a woman."

This nonsense, Holmes, is why people think you're a misogynist. Holmes has the opportunity to do something very noble, even if, as Windibank claims, there is nothing "actionable" about the situation, and yet he does nothing at all. He allows Mary Sutherland to live her life out with the impossible dream that her lover will return, and by that permits Mr. and Mrs. Windibank to get away with their scheme. He *allows it to work*.

In so many other stories, Holmes's approach is, "that strange/creepy man should not be doing that thing to you; let's stop him" (see SOLI, COPP, ILLU, LADY, SUSS, etc). Why in this one is his conclusion the Victorian equivalent of a shrug emoji? Now, this story an early one, so his character as a protector of the weak is not yet fully formed; perhaps his creator realized his mistake and took pains to adjust it in later works. One likes to imagine Watson, just after the final scene, putting his pen down and taking Holmes to task for his bad decision, and/or rushing out the door to tell Miss Sutherland himself. Holmes is shown in an unfavorable light in this story (but not in a sexy, cool way like with Irene Adler); Mary Sutherland deserves better.

Joan Watson
by Melinda Caric

You can count me among the legions of existing Sherlock fans that were more than a bit skeptical when *Elementary* was announced. For a while Sherlock Holmes was like the new zombie apocalypse (which was the new vampires): a resurrected topic with a bandwagon large enough for multiple networks, writers, and other creative hopefuls to throw themselves on. *Elementary* just seemed too gimmicky: hot on the heels of Sherlock, it tried to change up the characters and setting enough to differentiate itself while still capitalizing on the recent uptick in the popularity of the canon. I wanted it to be good, but my expectations were very low. It seemed unnecessary to move the characters to New York, the new Watson was so radically different from the character I knew as to be borderline unrecognizable, I was convinced that this was a cheap way to create a romance between Holmes and Watson, and I couldn't for the life of me understand why they didn't just make the damn show and give the leads different names, like Sherrinford and Sacker.

When the pilot finally aired, I still didn't see the point of it. I watched the first four episodes and wrote the whole thing off. It wasn't bad, but it wasn't exactly good either, and I've got better things to do with my time than waste an hour every week watching something that I don't feel passionate about.

Bending the gender of a character is nothing new, à la Katee Sackhoff as a female Starbuck in the *Battlestar Galactica* reboot. I realize I'm about to draw the collective ire of the entire internet, but I thought the treatment of her character was all wrong: she always appeared to be trying too hard, she always had something to prove, and in my opinion this made her totally unbelievable.

Luckily for me I have friends that stuck with the show and told me to give it another go. I figured Lucy Liu would be handed one of two roles: a new Kara Thrace constantly throwing her weight around, or a more typical Watson, passive and admiring and serving as a foil to Sherlock's quips.

Incredibly enough we didn't get either one of these things, and while it is difficult for me to pick a favorite Watson, Lucy Liu now comes first to mind. Her Watson is effortless. She's tough without resorting to bullying, intelligent without having to show off, and stands up for herself without appearing to be on a crusade. She understands that respect is earned rather than freely given, and never allows herself to be the recipient of abuse in any form.

For the first time that I can recall, Watson was treated as Holmes's equal, someone competent with talents worth developing and worthy of his respect. And she continues to impress me the more we get to see of her: she keeps her cool under extraordinary pressure, is constantly working to improve herself, has proven herself to be a fearless and invaluable asset to their partnership, stands her ground and fights back when faced with misogyny, and she calls Sherlock out on his shit – something that has been sorely lacking in the majority of adaptations. The esteem in which Holmes holds her is a real testament to how highly he thinks of her, and it is incredibly refreshing to see a Holmes/Watson relationship where the admiration goes both ways.

We are all familiar with seeing Holmes treat Watson as a sidekick, making disparaging remarks about his intelligence and abilities in an offhand and completely shitty way. *Elementary* removed this dynamic from the relationship and introduced us to two lead characters of equal ability – one the master of his finely honed craft, and the other no less capable but merely lacking in training. In many ways this strikes me as a show about Joan Watson rather than Sherlock Holmes, and she is certainly a character worth watching.

What impresses me about this particular adaptation is that despite the unorthodox casting Watson is treated as a human being, first and foremost: the fact that she is an American woman of color is completely arbitrary to her character. Watson was written as a modern individual rather than a Victorian character update, and then the best actor was cast for the role, race and color be damned.

We've come a long way from the simpering Nigel Bruce and the invisible Ian Hart. This new Watson is vibrant, essential, and one bad ass bitch. We salute you, Joan Watson, for making the everyman the most capable and competent everywoman we could have hoped for.

Kate Whitney
by Susanne Wagner

Kate Whitney probably cannot be considered the most luminous or fascinating female character in the Sherlock Holmes canon (and neither in the *Sherlock* BBC series, for that matter). She is not exactly a heroine or an interesting antagonist or even the classic "damsel in distress" client for Sherlock Holmes. But that does not mean that her character does not serve a purpose when it comes to the development of the story.

At the beginning of the canonical short story "The Man with the Twisted Lip," Kate Whitney is introduced to the reader as an old school friend of Dr. Watson's wife Mary. The *Sherlock Holmes* canon does not provide very much insight into the married life of the Watsons, so it is rather a rarity for the reader to meet them both at home. They are having a quiet domestic evening that is suddenly interrupted when an obviously distressed Kate Whitney arrives unexpectedly, looking for "a little help":

Her husband, Isa Whitney, an opium addict, has not been home for two days and she is convinced that he can be found in a particular opium den, the so called "Bar of Gold." This is a place though, where she, a "young and timid woman," cannot go alone and therefore needs Dr. Watson to escort here there, to "pluck her husband out from among the ruffians."

By the way: In the BBC's *Sherlock* adaptation we meet her as the mother of drug-addict ("shooting up" in this case) Isaac Whitney. She is turning to John and Mary for help, because her son has not returned home. Other than that, there is no significant difference between her character here and the one in the canon, so I am only adding that reference for the sake of completeness. Again, regarding the canon, I don't consider Kate Whitney a very interesting character as such, and not even particularly necessary for the plot. But what I do find interesting about her is how Arthur Conan Doyle deploys her to set the scene and mood for the actual story (i.e. the mystery). The first part is the domestic scene at the Watson's home, and their behavior towards Kate reflects very positively on them both: "Folk who were in grief came to my wife like birds to a light-house. [...] It was not the first time that she had spoken to us of her husband's trouble, to me as a doctor, to my wife as an old friend and school companion. We soothed and comforted her by such words as we could find."

From there the reader is led directly to the Bar of Gold (which, as we are bound to find out, happens to be one of the main settings of the subsequent mystery), where we not only meet the missing husband Isa Whitney (drugged and without an idea of how much time has passed since he left home) but also Sherlock Holmes in disguise. Watson takes care of Whitney, settles his debt with the opium den's owner, and puts him into a cab home to his wife (or "poor little Kate", according to her husband), together with an appropriate and probably reassuring note. As far as the situation with the Whitneys is concerned, that is the end of that story line, while for Holmes and Watson the game is afoot once more.

We do not know what will become of Kate and Isa Whitney. Will this be the last time that Kate has to worry about the "orgies" of her husband? Is it possible that this incident has been, finally, the point where Isa understands that he needs to get a grip on his addiction, and be it only because he realizes just how much he has been hurting his wife? This might be material for further speculation, but within the canon, we do not receive an answer to that question. It is reasonable to suppose that Kate will forgive her husband, just as it is likely that Mrs. St. Clair, the actual client in this story, will forgive her own husband for the trouble and anguish he has put her through – even though the reasons are not quite the same. (Still, in some aspects there are several parallels between the two women.)

Kate Whitney appears as an almost archetypical character – the loving, loyal, long-suffering wife – and certainly represents an aspect of the middle/upper class Victorian lady, the role she plays within her family and society, as well as the constraints this role imposes upon her.

In the circle of women of the Sherlock Holmes canon she might be easily overlooked – so maybe it is time to give her some appreciation.

Kitty Winter
by Lyndsay Faye

Sherlock Holmes is as reliable on the subject of his own opinions regarding females as John Watson is about trifling matters like chronology. No, seriously – they're both equally skilled humans when it comes to communicating their own facts. Take, just to preface this piece, Holmes on the subject of women:

"Women are never to be entirely trusted – not the best of them." (*The Sign of Four*)

"Puurrr scritch knead hsssss prrrrrrrr, you are so awesome I can't stand it, let's be pals forever." (*Actual [Paraphrased] Sherlock Holmes Behavior with Several Women from the Canon*)

Sherlock Holmes treats women just as he treats men, for the most part – well, when he thinks them honorable, poorly, when he thinks them duplicitous. Meanwhile, nowhere does Sherlock Holmes prove himself more of a gallant pussycat than when it comes to Kitty Winter, as he clearly takes every measure he can to shield her from the long arm of the law.

But this isn't about Sherlock Holmes, and I have a confession to make. My Baker Street Irregulars investiture (unexpected when it came, cherished today) is Kitty Winter. I am not the first to carry this ferocious nomenclature. ASH, BSI Maureen Green was the original, and she tragically passed before I had the opportunity of meeting her. I regret this as I wander about with her pseudonym, hoping she approves posthumously. Additionally, Kitty as a character (and as an emblem of the population of females she embodies) is very important to me in other ways, so let's talk about those.

Let's talk about slut-shaming for a second, shall we? Don't do it. Sherlock Holmes didn't, so why should we?

If you're clutching your pearls right now, read no further, because Sherlock "Misogynist" Holmes behaved in a much more civilized manner. "The Illustrious Client" emphatically resides in my top five canonical cases for several reasons. One is that we very seldom see Holmes miscalculate, so it is something of a bitter pleasure to watch his ass being handed to him after sassing five too many thugs (or simply the wrong thug, the "unlucky" thug, the one named Baron Adelbert Gruner). When heroes are too complacent or too competent, we lose interest, so Holmes's fallibility in this instance is extremely valuable in the storytelling sense. Far more interesting to me, however, is the way in which he treats Kitty Winter.

During the Victorian era, it was supposedly thought decorous to cover the legs of tables lest improper thoughts arise, whilst concurrently, wicked dirty sloppy epic porn was being written (and published), probably because people thought hovercraft tables were weird and were hoping for a mahogany stem from time to time so they could picture a clawfoot ottoman when wanking in the shower. I figure people can already parse my thoughts on hypocrisy at this point, so I'll stick to hard data. Women fell into five categories, so far as I can tell: virtuous youth, virtuous matron/widow, not-white-so-you-don't-count, wife, and whore.

Sherlock Holmes in "The Illustrious Client" is consulted upon an unlikely topic, as I'm fairly sure he abhors domestic squabbles and wishes he could confine himself entirely to locked rooms: Baron Gruner is about to marry Violet de Merville, a beautiful (and rich) and poised (and rich) woman whose male chaperones think it might be a bad idea for her to marry a dude who almost certainly shanked his exes. This might have devolved pretty quickly into a revolting moral fable, but when Sherlock Holmes agrees that Violet ought not expose herself to quite so many shivs, he brings in a survivor of the identical abuse: one Kitty Winter.

Violet is set up by the men in the consulting room as being nine hundred percent cray-cray: "To say that she loves him hardly expresses it. She dotes upon him; she is obsessed by him. Outside of him there is nothing on earth. She will not hear one word against him," reports Colonel Damery, who gives us a clue as to the state of the sitting room by refusing to remove his gloves for the entire interview.

Holmes initially declines to approach the potential victim in person. Instead, he visits Gruner, warns him off, is warned off in turn, and reports back to Watson. I will paraphrase his summary of these events with the words, "I Visited Baron Gruner's Chinese Pottery Barn and Snuff Sex Shoppe, And All I Got Was This Shitty T-Shirt."

Enter Kitty Winter. In Watson's words, Shinwell Johnson was seated and:

> [...] beside him on the settee was a brand which he had brought up in the shape of a slim, flame-like young woman with a pale, intense face, youthful, and yet so worn with sin and sorrow that one read the terrible years which had left their leprous mark upon her.

So Kitty Winter is a hooker.

Let's make no bones about this. We are as close as we ever, ever, ever come here to Doyle mentioning "unfortunates" existed. Why is Kitty Winter a fallen woman? She hasn't done anything wrong, not that we know of. She seems a kind, intelligent, wryly funny person. When indirectly asked how she was found, Kitty quips, "[h]ell, London, gets me every time." Her suburb is clearly uncomfortable, her occupation the eldest one, her mind sharp and her sass factor off the charts. Sherlock Holmes is meant to be squirrelly around the ladyfolk, meanwhile, and might presumably have shied away from this Jezebel: "Holmes smiled. 'I gather we have your good wishes, Miss Winter.'"

Nah. Holmes is fine.

"'[...] well, there, she'll speak for herself,'" Shinwell "Porky" Johnson avers.

If I were left to my own devices entirely, I'd quote everything Kitty Winter said throughout the entire case, but that would prove inefficient. First off, she sits there in this room full of men – a nark, a consulting detective, and an army doctor – and tells them without any trace of shame that Baron Gruner ruined her. She mentions, "Porky Shinwell has been telling me. He's after some other poor fool and wants to marry her this time." Baron Gruner never offered to marry Kitty. She's confessing to three Victorian men that she had sex with the Baron and he hadn't even proposed. She loved him, so she slept with him – that's what Kitty has admitted in the Baker Street sitting room. Does Holmes throw her to the curb? No.

Holmes asks her, very courteously, what more she can tell them. And she answers:

'I tell you, Mr. Holmes, this man collects women, and takes a pride in his collection, as some men collect moths or butterflies. He had it all in that book. Snapshot photographs, names, details, everything about them. It was a beastly book – a book no man, even if he had come from the gutter, could have put together. But it was Adelbert Gruner's book all the same. 'Souls I have ruined.' He could have put that on the outside if he had been so minded.'

You can call Gruner whatever you like. Call him a serial murderer, a philanderer, a liar, a killer, a fiend, a brute eager to trample anyone in his path. Whatever you call him, Kitty Winter had the guts to say she'd face down his fiancée as a last resort, and when Holmes offers to pay her for this service:

'None of that, Mr. Holmes,' cried the young woman. 'I am not out for money. Let me see this man in the mud, and I've got all I've worked for – in the mud with my foot on his cursed face. That's my price. I'm with you to-morrow or any other day so long as you are on his track.'

What a woman, as some have said. What a woman! Sir Arthur Conan Doyle was passionate on the subject of divorce reform, as well he should have been. Holmes in an uncannily Doyle-like voice protests to Violet de Merville:

'But I really did plead with her with all the warmth of words that I could find in my nature. I pictured to her the awful position of the woman who only wakes to a man's character after she is his wife – a woman who has to submit to be caressed by bloody hands and lecherous lips. I spared her nothing – the shame, the fear, the agony, the hopelessness of it all.'

Of course this doesn't work, but Kitty does Holmes one better. This is one of the most striking feminist passages in the entire canon, because Kitty gives zero fucks about Violet, but she's there to say her piece anyhow, and meanwhile Holmes has **brought a whore to show-and-**

tell to serve as his evidence, so we are already waaaaaaaaaaaay outside the land of shrouded table legs here:

> 'I am his last mistress. I am one of a hundred that he has tempted and used and ruined and thrown into the refuse heap, as he will you also. Your refuse heap is more likely to be a grave, and maybe that's the best. I tell you, you foolish woman, if you marry this man he'll be the death of you. It may be a broken heart or it may be a broken neck, but he'll have you one way or the other. It's not out of love for you I'm speaking. I don't care a tinker's curse whether you live or die. It's out of hate for him and to spite him and to get back on him for what he did to me. But it's all the same, and you needn't look at me like that, my fine lady, for you may be lower than I am before you are through with it.'

Later in the case, highly dramatic events occur. Holmes is beaten to a pulp, Watson is devastated, Gruner gloats, and Kitty ends up throwing vitriol in her persecutor's smug face. Most tellingly, I think, Holmes is severely injured in act three, and he then enlists allies. Of course he assigns Watson the essential role of affable decoy – Watson was practically gnashing his teeth over Holmes's sickbed, which is lovely in its own right. But then **Sherlock Holmes brings Kitty along with him to burgle the house**.

Clearly, Holmes thinks she might know where the lust diary is. But it doesn't matter to him that she lives in Hell, London. It doesn't matter that she's a prostitute. It doesn't matter that she rode Baron Bruner like a rodeo cowboy when only men were meant to have sex drives. Sherlock Holmes gives nil shits on all of these topics. And I appreciate that, because I adore Kitty Winter. And I would argue that – despite his nasty comments on the subject of hairpins and curling-tongs – Sherlock Holmes did too.

A NOTE ON THE ILLUSTRATIONS

Illustrations on the following pages are in the common domain, created by Sidney Paget for *The Strand Magazine* publications of the *Sherlock Holmes* stories: 13, 22, 31, 42, 51, 69, 78, 84, 91, 93 and 95.

Illustrations on the following pages are by Merilyn Paugus: 3, 17, 39, 48 and 65. All rights belong to her.

The screenshots on page 46 belong to Granada Television (*The Musgrave Ritual*, 1 February 1988).

The illustration on page 22 is by Howard K. Elcock (*The Strand Magazine,* January 1924) and also in the common domain.

The cover was created by Maria Fleischhack.

www.ingramcontent.com/pod-product-compliance
Lightning Source LLC
Chambersburg PA
CBHW070046210526
45170CB00012B/601